DO We NEED A NEW CONSTITUTION?

GERALD LEINWAND

Democracy in Action
Franklin Watts
New York/Chicago/London/Toronto/Sydney

Library of Congress Cataloging-in-Publication Data

Leinwand, Gerald.
Do we need a new Constitution? / Gerald Leinwand.
p. cm.—(Democracy in action)
Includes bibliographical references and index.
ISBN 0-531-11127-X
1. United States—Constitutional law—Juvenile literature. 2. Law
reform—United States—Juvenile literature. I. Title. II. Series.
KF4550.Z9L42   1944
342.73'02—dc20   93-31847   CIP AC
[347.3022]

"It is written: For every right that you cherish, you have a duty which you must fulfill. For every hope that you entertain, you have a task you must perform. For every good that you wish to preserve, you will have to sacrifice your comfort and your ease. There is nothing for nothing any longer."

—Walter Lippmann to the Harvard Class of 1940. Quoted in David S. Broder, *The Party's Over: The Failure of Politics in America.* New York: Harper and Row Publishers, 1971, p. 264.

CONTENTS

PROLOGUE

As Americans prepared to go to the polls in November 1992, they did so with little confidence that the future, for themselves and for their country, would be as bright as it had been in the past. Rightly or wrongly, they were worried that their children might not live as well as they had, and that America had somehow lost its clout as a strong nation.

While President Ronald Reagan boldly proclaimed that it was "Morning in America," many Americans felt that the future would not be as productive as the past. In a *New York Times/CBS News* poll taken in the latter part of 1992, 46 percent of those polled felt that future generations of Americans would be worse off, 26 percent felt that they would be better off, while only 19 percent believed that the future for Americans would be about the same as today.[1] In 1991, 73 percent of Americans polled felt that there were greater global challenges to America's economic standing, and that the most difficult period for Americans lay ahead.[2]

Today, the Constitution is a revered icon of America and stands as much as a symbol of the nation as it does the framework of government. But does such reverence mean that the Constitution may not be changed? Is the American Constitution, written more than two hundred years ago, adequate for the needs of the nation for generations to come?

Thomas Jefferson, one of the Founding Fathers but not a framer of the Constitution (he was United States minister to France at the time), regarded the document less reverentially. In 1816 he wrote:

> *Some men look at constitutions with sanctimonious reverence, and deem them like the arc [sic] of the covenant, too sacred to be touched. They ascribe to the men of the preceding age a wisdom more than human, and suppose what they did to be beyond amendment. I knew that age well; I belonged to it, and labored with it; it deserved well of its country. It was very like the present, but without the experience of the present; and forty years of experience in government is worth a century of book-reading; and this they would say themselves were they to rise from the dead.*

The framers of the Constitution understood that change might be needed but adopted a cumbersome method of amending, or making these changes. Is the amending process enough to make the Constitution responsive to a nation that is radically different from the one the framers of the Constitution experienced? Does the Constitution need such massive repairs that a new constitutional convention needs to be convened? And, if another constitutional convention is called for, would it be better to draft an altogether new document? If a new constitution is written and adopted, do we have any assurance that it will be better than the system of government which has served us so well for so long?

In the pages that follow, we will briefly review

how the Constitution was written, examine the framework of government it created, explore some of the shortcomings of our political system, and set forth the the pros and cons of the need for a new constitution.

On the basis of the arguments presented in this volume should another constitutional convention be called? Should it revise the Constitution or should it write a new one? You will be asked to think about these questions.

Gerald Leinwand
New York City, 1994

TOWARD A MORE PERFECT UNION

"Like the Bible, it ought to be read again and again. It is an easy document to understand."[1] So declared President Franklin D. Roosevelt in a radio address in March 1937 during one of his "fireside chats" with the American people.

President Roosevelt was only partly right. While it ought to be read, the Constitution is not easy to understand. It is full of ambiguities. If you were to read the Constitution of the United States, you would have some idea of how the framers of that document intended the new government to work, but it would be difficult to tell from that document alone how America is actually governed. For in addition to the written Constitution there is something known as the "unwritten Constitution," made up of a body of traditions and practices and laws and judicial decisions that are not referred to in the Constitution at all. The political party system, the way presidents are nominated, the judicial review of laws, the committee system of Congress, and the administrative structure of the White House are among those aspects of our government that are not mentioned in the Constitution.

While the Constitution is a document that tells us

something, but not everything, about how America is governed, it has also become a venerated symbol of the nation. Is it a sacred text that we change only at our peril, or is it an instrument of government that we may change periodically to meet our needs? In order to consider these questions, in this chapter we will examine the essential features of the government the Constitution created more than 200 years ago.

WRITING
THE UNITED STATES
CONSTITUTION
The idea of drafting a Constitution came naturally to the people who assembled in Philadelphia in 1787. After all, during America's colonial experience, the Pilgrims who settled in Massachusetts had written the Mayflower Compact (1620) even before their vessel reached what their leader, William Bradford, described as "a harsh and desolate wilderness." The Fundamental Orders of Connecticut (1639) and Penn's Frame of Government (1682) are other noteworthy examples of early colonial constitutions.

Of more immediate importance were the state constitutions that were framed or at least revised in 1776, when the Declaration of Independence (See Appendix A) announced that the thirteen colonies intended to separate from England. The constitutions written, for example, in 1776 for Virginia and drafted in 1780 for Massachusetts, are striking forerunners of both the content and the principles upon which the Constitution of the United States was later framed. Although the state constitutions were not models in every respect, by writing them and by trying to enforce their provisions, the Founding Fathers learned something about how America might best be governed. However, in spite of these experiences, the first attempt to draft a constitution for the United States of America was a failure.

In order to put into practice the ideals set forth in the Declaration of Independence, the Articles of Confederation were drafted; they served as the first constitution of the United States from 1781 to 1789. Among the major features were:

- *Each state, retaining sovereignty (supreme power) and having one vote, was to be represented in Congress.*
- *Congress could declare war, stamp metal coins and print paper money, regulate weights and measures, borrow funds, negotiate treaties with foreign countries, regulate Indian affairs, raise and equip a military, and make treaties.*
- *Agreement by nine states was required to pass laws.*
- *Unanimous consent of all the states was required to change the Articles.*

The preamble to the Articles of Confederation described the new nation as only "a firm league of friendship." The central government had no presidency, no judiciary, no power to regulate foreign and domestic commerce, and no taxing power of its own. It could only appeal to the states for the money it needed to function and, as often as not, the states refused to be generous.

In spite of these handicaps, the government under the Articles of Confederation did accomplish some good things. The most important of these was the Northwest Ordinance of 1787 which provided for the government of the lands relinquished by several seaboard states and known as the old Northwest (northwest of the Ohio River, east of the Mississippi River, and south of the Great Lakes). The Ordinance provided that when these areas grew to 60,000 in population, they could be admitted by Congress as a state with privileges equal to those of the original states. This piece of legislation was farsighted; Congress could have insisted that the lands of the Old

Northwest be thought of as a colony to be ruled by Congress as the thirteen colonies had been ruled by England. By ensuring that this would not happen, the growth of the new nation was assured. However, in spite of some important achievements, by 1787 the new nation was near anarchy.

Among foreign countries, the new nation received little respect. Britain, the mother country, was understandably unfriendly. When John Adams, minister to Great Britain, sought to establish a commercial treaty, British Foreign Secretary Charles James Fox derisively suggested that Congress lacked treaty-making authority. Spain sought much of the new nation's land along the Mississippi and so was hostile. France, an ally in the American Revolution, feared the growth of republicanism, and became unfriendly. Pirates along the Barbary coast of North Africa were attacking American merchant ships and enslaving its sailors.

In addition to the new American government appearing powerless to the strong nations abroad, the thirteen states were having problems with the powers of the new Congress as well. They complained about "King Congress" and argued among themselves about tariffs and borders. Moreover, each state could and did impose a tax on goods coming from other states. New York, for example, taxed firewood coming from Connecticut and cabbages coming from New Jersey. Some states were printing their own money, thus making such "rag money" nearly worthless.

The nation's credit was deteriorating, soldiers of the American Revolution had not been paid, the national debt was mounting, and money was becoming valueless. In some of the rural parts of the country, farms were being foreclosed, that is, taken away from their owners for failure to pay debts, at a rapid rate.

Since imprisonment for debt was common in those days, many farmers were jailed.

Symbolic of the mounting dissatisfaction of the people was a rebellion in western Massachusetts by bands of farmers led by revolutionary war hero Captain Daniel Shays. At Northampton and Springfield, bands of indebted farmers, some armed with muskets, refused to let the courts meet so that indebted farmers would not have their lands taken from them or be imprisoned for debt. Under Massachusetts's Governor James Bowdoin, what appeared to be armed insurrection was met with force. A loyal state militia dispersed the rebels, but not before more than thirty of the protesting farmers had been killed. Some fled to Canada; Daniel Shays was condemned to death (he was later pardoned). Shays's Rebellion was crushed, but people of property were afraid that the new government could not protect either them or their property. Clearly, a new and stronger government would be needed.

As a result of these difficulties at home and abroad, many people, especially in the middle and upper classes, felt the need for a strong central government. Some even considered the possibility of a king. Under the influence of James Madison of Virginia and Alexander Hamilton of New York, state representatives met at Alexandria, Virginia, to settle a dispute between Maryland and Virginia over commerce on the Potomac River. The meeting also addressed the wider problems of the nation. At George Washington's invitation the meeting was moved to his home at Mount Vernon, Virginia, where the representatives of the two states hammered out an agreement. If Virginia and Maryland could settle their differences in this way, perhaps a meeting of all the states would settle the differences in the nation as a whole.

The Virginia legislature called for a meeting at Annapolis, Maryland, to iron out trade and commerce problems among all the states. Only five states sent representatives to Annapolis. The meeting was a short but important one. Those who met at Annapolis asked that a convention of all states review the Articles of Confederation. There was substantial enthusiasm from most, but not all, for this idea. The delegates met in Philadelphia in May 1787 to amend the Articles. But they were to go farther than they expected—they were to write a new constitution.

On May 25, 1787, the Constitutional Convention began its deliberations. During the course of the debate, fifty-five delegates representing twelve states took part. Only Rhode Island sent no representative. Those who assembled were among the ablest men in the nation. George Washington chaired the meetings with patience and tact. Benjamin Franklin was the convention's oldest member and its most experienced. Alexander Hamilton was there to urge the creation of a strong central government. James Madison was probably the most knowledgeable of those assembled. He had studied governments of the past and knew the principles upon which sound government might be built. For his work at the convention and for the notes he took, Madison is called the "Father of the Constitution."

Many heroes of the Revolution such as John Adams, Samuel Adams, Thomas Jefferson, and Thomas Paine did not attend. Patrick Henry, who in the Virginia House of Burgesses had been among the first to flirt with treason when he attacked British laws, would not come. He "smelt a Rat," he said. He had guessed that the Articles of Confederation, which he preferred, would be scrapped and a new constitution written.

Of the men at the convention, Madison wrote:

"There never was an assembly of men, charged with a great and arduous trust, who were more pure in their motives or more exclusively or anxiously devoted to the object committed to them."[2] However, it was in the interest of most of those present to have a strong central government. Nearly all the men at the convention came from the well-to-do class. They were merchants and large landowners. They were financiers, planters, soldiers, and holders of high office. They were well-educated. Half were lawyers. Most of them were young men with conservative leanings who sought to establish a government that could deal with someone like Daniel Shays. They wanted a government that would pay its debts, provide a stable currency, and force debtors to pay what they owed. They held government bonds and wanted to be sure that they would be repaid.

The convention, right from the start, made two important decisions. One was to keep the debates secret. The other was to discard the Articles of Confederation and draft a new constitution. What kind of constitution would they write?

After a long summer of hard work and heated debate, thirty-nine delegates signed the document on September 17, 1787. The framers of the Constitution recognized that what they had drafted was by no means a perfect document. They understood that by following its provisions the new nation was embarking on a bold experiment, not a sure thing. In a speech read for him by James Wilson, the elderly, pain-racked Benjamin Franklin confessed that while there were several parts of the Constitution he did not approve of, he accepted this Constitution "because I expect no better, and because I am not sure that it is not the best."

The Constitution was to go into effect when it had been ratified, or approved, by special conventions in

17

any nine of the thirteen states. This procedure had no legal precedent, since the amending procedure under the Articles of Confederation required unanimous consent. Only the critical nature of the times and the fact that the Constitution was a new creation rather than a revision, justified this method of ratification. The people were, however, given an indirect voice in determining whether the new Constitution was to become the supreme law of the land.

The debate over ratification led to the formation of America's first political parties. Those who favored ratification were the Federalists, led by Madison, Hamilton, and Washington. In general, they sought a strong central government with vast authority over taxes, interstate commerce, and the military. Those who opposed ratification were the Anti-Federalists, eventually led by Jefferson, who feared the arbitrary power of a strong central government and preferred strong state governments.

Mercy Otis Owen who, along with Abigail Adams, was one of the very few women who participated in the debate over the Constitution, expressed the views of the Anti-Federalists. Under the pseudonym "A Columbian Patriot," Mercy Otis Owen blisteringly attacked "the many-headed monster" of the central government that the Constitutional Convention was submitting to the people for ratification. It would become, she said, "the nursery of vice and the bane of liberty."[3] Fears similar to those expressed by Mercy Owen made the debate over ratification a vigorous one and adoption by no means assured.

To the Americans of those days, the structure of government appeared less important than assurances that their liberties would be protected. It was, after all, to worship as they wished and to govern themselves that they had come to America's shores, and they saw little in the Constitution that would adequately protect them. Not until a Bill of Rights guaranteeing individual liberties was promised to them was the Constitution narrowly ratified.

By June 1788, nine states had ratified the Constitution and adoption seemed almost certain. But since the key states of Virginia and New York had not yet ratified it, the birth of the new nation was not completely assured. It was no easy task to oppose Patrick Henry in Virginia, but with the help of Washington and Madison the Constitution was finally approved by ten votes.

In New York, the contest between the Federalists, who favored ratification, and the Anti-Federalists, who opposed it, was especially close. Hamilton, Madison, and John Jay (who later became the nation's first Chief Justice) published a series of anonymous newspaper articles urging adoption of the Constitution. Eighty-five articles were printed and later published as *The Federalist*. They remain today a vital source for the basic principles that guided the Founding Fathers. The articles in *The Federalist* were probably responsible for the three-vote margin of victory by which New York accepted the Constitution.

About ten o'clock in the morning, April 16, 1789, George Washington climbed into a carriage standing outside his home in Mount Vernon to begin the journey to the nation's capital in New York City to assume the office of president of the United States. Short of cash because of a poor tobacco harvest, he borrowed money for the journey. He had not sought the presidency, but he was prepared to accept the call of the nation. In a driving rain he gave his Inaugural Address. He prayed to the "Almighty Being who rules over the Universe. . . . [that] the experiment entrusted to the hands of the American people . . ." would succeed.[4] The first president had good reason to be anxious. Without precedents to guide him, he would be the first to preside over an experiment in self-government.

In the words of the Preamble to the Constitution of the United States, "We, the people of the United States, in order to form a more perfect Union, establish justice, insure domestic tranquility, provide for the common defence, promote the general Welfare, and secure the blessings of liberty to ourselves and our posterity, do ordain and establish this Constitution for the United States of America." But was the Constitution a compact of the states or of the people? Would an untested document create a "more perfect Union"? Was it possible to establish justice for all, insure domestic tranquility, and provide for the common defense? Above all, what was the general welfare and how could the general welfare best be promoted? What does it mean to secure the blessings of liberty? Whose liberty? What if liberties clash with one another? And, how far into the future should the principles of the Constitution guide us? The framers of the Constitution did their work well, but they would probably be surprised that the Constitution, with few changes, has lasted as long and served the country as well as it has.

The basic principles upon which the experiment in self-government was to be based may be summarized as follows:

1. Can a republican form of government succeed?

When Americans salute the flag, they pledge allegiance "to the flag of the United States of America and to the republic for which it stands." A republic is a government that has no king and in which representatives of the people govern. In 1789, this was a daring departure from the monarchial form of government that prevailed everywhere else. While all countries in those days were ruled by hereditary monarchs, America had an elected president at its head.

The Founding Fathers provided for a republic, not a democracy. According to the Constitution, the people were to vote only for members of the House of Representatives. The right to vote was determined by each state, and most states limited the vote to white male property owners. The members of the United States Senate would be elected by the legislatures of the states; the president would be named by a group of prominent people chosen in any manner decided upon by the state legislatures. This group, later called the Electoral College, was to choose the president of the United States. The members of the Supreme Court were to be appointed by the president.

A republic becomes a democracy when the right to vote is widely held, when two or more political parties exist, and when freedom of speech, press, religion, and assembly are guaranteed. Only over the course of more than 200 years did the republic of 1789 become the democracy of today. Keeping and enhancing democracy remains a challenge for each generation of Americans.

2. *Can a federal system of government be effective?*

A federal system is one in which, as in the United States, power is divided between the national government and the state governments. In such a system a person has dual citizenship. That is, a person is a citizen of the nation and also of the state in which he or she lives. The Constitution gave specifically expressed, or enumerated, powers to the national government. These are spelled out in Article I, Section 8 of the Constitution and include the power to "lay and collect taxes, borrow and coin money, declare war, maintain a military, regulate interstate commerce . . ." as well as a number of others. To the states it gave reserved, or residual, powers; those powers not granted to Congress nor denied to the states belong to the states. The residual powers of the states were reinforced in Amendment X of the Bill of Rights, which reads: "The powers not delegated to the United States by the Constitution, nor prohibited by it to the States, are reserved to the States respectively, or to the people."

Because federalism invites conflict between national and state governments, the framers of the Constitution in Article VI, Section 2 provided that in any conflicts between state and national laws, the national law passed under the Constitution would be supreme. Moreover, states were forbidden to maintain standing armies, make treaties with foreign powers, or coin money.

3. *Would separation of powers lead to gridlock in government?*

The federal government consists of three separate branches. The legislative or law-making branch called Congress is made up of a lower house, the House of Representatives, and an upper house called the Senate. The House of Representatives has 435 members who are elected for two-year terms. The Senate has two senators from each state, for a total of 100 members who serve for six years. For a law to be passed by Congress, both the House and the Senate must approve by majority vote and the president must sign.

The executive power is vested in the president who may, with the advice and consent of the Senate, appoint a cabinet and other agencies of government. The president can veto bills passed by Congress, but the veto can be overridden by a two-thirds vote of each house of Congress. The president also conducts foreign policy and makes treaties subject to a two-thirds vote of the Senate.

The judicial power, the Supreme Court and the lower federal courts, interprets the law. The members of the United States Supreme Court are appointed by the president and must be approved by more than half of the Senate.

By establishing three separate branches of government, the Founding Fathers set up a system of checks and balances by which one branch of government could prevent the other branches from becoming too powerful or exercising arbitrary control. This system of checks and balances is one of the constitutional safeguards against tyranny.

Thus, to guard against tyranny the Constitution provided for a federal system in which power is divided between the states and the nation, and for separation of powers among the three branches of government.

4. *Is judicial review an adequate safeguard of American liberties?*

"We live under a Constitution," Justice Charles Evans Hughes declared in 1907, "but the Constitution is what the judges say it is." Because justices are appointed for life by the president, the president can appoint justices who share his or her views on government, liberty, and religious and political freedom. These justices can still be in place long after the president has left office. The Judiciary Act of September 24, 1789, breathed life into the constitutional provisions for a federal judiciary. A federal judicial pyramid was created consisting of a Supreme Court (made up of a chief justice and five associate justices), a United States Circuit Court of Appeals, and federal district courts.

Along with federalism, judicial review is a uniquely American contribution to the art of government. Regarded by the framers as the weakest of the three branches of government, the doctrine of judicial review, although not explicitly provided for in the Constitution, has made the federal judicial system at least as powerful as the legislative and executive branches of government and perhaps even more so.

The Supreme Court is mainly a court of appellate jurisdiction—cases reach the highest court of the land only through appeal from other state or federal courts. The Supreme Court has original jurisdiction in cases affecting ambassadors and public ministers, and in cases to which a state is a party. Today, the Supreme Court is made up of a chief justice and eight associate justices all appointed by the president and approved by the Senate of the United States.

The Supreme Court first exercised its power of declaring a law of Congress unconstitutional in the celebrated case of *Marbury v. Madison* (1803) when it declared a portion of the Judiciary Act of 1789 unconstitutional. By asserting its right to review acts of Congress, of state legislatures, and of lower courts, the Supreme Court exercised its power of judicial review. This set an extremely important precedent that made the Supreme Court a powerful branch of the federal government. Because of the pivotal position the Supreme Court has occupied at crucial points in the nation's history, it has sometimes been called "the balance wheel of the republic."

SOME MYTHS AND TRUTHS ABOUT THE CONSTITUTION

The convention called to write the Constitution was unique in America's history, and its framers have become enshrined as national heroes. But this venerated document has been shaped as much by myth as by truth. In the last article in *The Federalist* No. 85, Alexander Hamilton urged that the Constitution be adopted in spite of its imperfections. "I never expected to see a perfect work from imperfect man,"[5] he wrote. Because myth has obscured some of the imperfections in the document, a brief summary of some of the myths and truths can help us see the Constitution in a clearer perspective.

Myth: Those who assembled at Philadelphia in 1787 were authorized to draft a *new* Constitution for the United States of America.

Truth: Congress only reluctantly agreed to a convention to be held "for the sole and express purpose of revising the Articles of Confederation." A convention had been called to improve upon the old document, not write a new one. "It is easy to forget that the Philadelphia Convention vastly exceeded its authority, and that the men who met there undertook what amounted to a usurpation of legitimate authority."[6] Legitimacy was given to the Constitution, however, by the process by which the document was ratified.

Myth: Those who met at Philadelphia were representative of the people.

Truth: They were not. For the most part, the able men who assembled at Philadelphia in the summer of 1787 had been chosen by the legislatures of their respective states rather than by votes of the people. They were experienced, and of the fifty-five who took part, thirty-one had been educated at colonial colleges or at similar institutions in Europe. There were two university presidents and three professors. There were lawyers and planters, men of business and of property. Most of these men were creditors, not debtors, and they sought to have the new nation help them collect the money due them. Moreover, many groups were not represented, including the more radical advocates of separation from England—Patrick Henry, Thomas Paine, Samuel Adams—all of whom feared the idea of a strong central government. From our perspective we recognize that there were also no women among them, no blacks, no indentured servants, no men without property, and no Indians.

Myth: The Constitution established a democracy.

Truth: It did not. We have already noted that the Constitution established a republican form of government (see page 25), not a democratic one. Only the House of Representatives was to be chosen by the people. Eligibility to vote was decided by the individual states, and initially only men of property could do so. The framers of the Constitution feared democracy, or what they viewed as rule by the mob. Franklin, who was at the convention, and Jefferson, who was not, were both more receptive to broad participation. The same cannot be said for most of those who drafted the Constitution. John Adams, who was abroad during the convention, described democracy as "the most ignoble, unjust and detestable form of government."[7] Lest we be too harsh on the framers of the Constitution it would be well to remember that "nowhere in America or Europe—not even among the great liberated thinkers . . . did democratic ideas appear respectable to the cultivated classes."[8]

Myth: The framers of the Constitution reconciled liberty and slavery.

Truth: Clearly, they did not. Slavery and the slave trade were discussed at the Constitutional Convention, and while some of the delegates favored abolishing slavery, they could not persuade representatives from the large slaveholding states, mainly Georgia and South Carolina, to agree. As the "price of union," the Constitution compromised with slavery and permitted the ownership in perpetuity of one person (a black) by another (a white). Although the slave trade was to be abolished by 1807, the decision of what to do about slavery itself was left to the states. Moreover, according to the formula for allocating representation in Congress and for direct taxation, each slave was to be counted as three-fifths of one person. Accommodating slavery meant that seventy-four years later the nation would have to deal with the issue in a bloody civil war.

The Constitution has often been described as a "living document" because over the centuries, despite its imperfections, it has been improved upon, and it has proved flexible enough to suit radically altered times. As the dawn of the twenty-first century approaches, will the Constitution be as accommodating to developments of the next hundred years as it has been to the past two hundred? If change and adaptation are needed, will they come peacefully or otherwise?

OUR FEDERAL SYSTEM: TOO MANY GOVERNMENTS OR TOO FEW?

Before a crowded courtroom on January 22, 1973, Justice Harry Blackmun summarized his decision in *Roe v. Wade*. By a 7–2 vote the United States Supreme Court had ruled that a state may not prevent women from having abortions during the first six months of pregnancy. This ruling invalidated the abortion laws in Texas and Georgia and, in effect, overturned restrictions in forty-four other states. Americans did not immediately realize the explosive nature of this decision.

Lyndon Johnson, the thirty-sixth president of the United States, died the same day, and the nation was riveted by preparations for his impressive funeral. A day later, a cease-fire in Vietnam was announced, and one could almost hear the collective sigh of relief that this unpopular war was at last drawing to a close. But the decision in *Roe v. Wade* would reveal a divisiveness in the nation matched only by the struggle over slavery and the Civil War itself.

In the more than twenty years since the *Roe v. Wade* decision, those who call themselves pro-life (people opposed to abortion altogether) and those who are pro-choice (people in favor of a woman's right to choose whether or not to give birth) have waged rigorous battles in the courts, in state legislatures, and in Congress. A conservative United States Supreme Court whittled away at *Roe v. Wade* but did not entirely overrule it.

As one of the first acts of the Clinton administration, the new president overturned the "gag" rule, a rule that made it illegal for federally funded family planning clinics to include abortion counseling as an option. The new president also proposed that federal Medicaid money be used to pay doctors to perform legal abortions for women who might otherwise be unable to afford one. Nevertheless, the struggle continues over the abortion issue. During protests outside abortion clinics, violent clashes sometimes take place when antiabortion groups seek to prevent patients' access. In 1993, in one of these demonstrations, an antiabortion demonstrator shot and killed a physician who preformed abortions. The legal battle over abortion will be waged in the courts, in Congress, and in the federal and state governments. This highly charged struggle over the propriety of abortion will shake the federal system to its very roots, much as the slavery question did over 130 years ago.

In the pages that follow we will review the nature of the relationships between the national and state governments. We will discuss some of the advantages and disadvantages of our federal system, trace the ebb and flow of state and federal power, and examine whether or not a federal system can be expected to be responsive to the needs of the nation in the next century.

OUR FEDERAL SYSTEM

Try to answer this question. A young couple, residents of New York, decide to marry in New Jersey. They return to New York to live and work. Is their marriage valid in New York? Here's another. A woman buys a car in Arizona and agrees to take three years to pay for it. During this period she moves to California to live. Can she be compelled to keep up the payments? If you answered "yes" to each of these questions you are correct.

While Article VI makes the Constitution and "the laws made in pursuance thereof," the supreme law of the land, Article IV, Section 1 of the Constitution requires that "full faith and credit shall be given in each state to the public acts, records, and judicial proceedings of every other state." This section means that contracts, wills, and similar documents drawn up in one state are legal in any of the other states. Thus, a marriage contract made in one state is valid in any of the fifty states. An agreement to pay for a car over a period of time is binding no matter where the purchaser lives.

Article IV, Section 2 of the Constitution provides that "the citizens of each state shall be entitled to all privileges and immunities of citizens in the several states." The "privileges and immunities" clause of the Constitution means that the people of one state may enjoy the same rights of person and property as the people of another state. No complete list of privileges and immunities exists, but among the more common ones determined by the courts from time to time are the right to buy or sell goods, the right to make contracts, and the right to travel through or to live in any state for pleasure, business, or professional purposes. A state may, however, impose voting residence requirements for newcomers.

However, certain functions that come under a state's police powers, those powers that enable the state to regulate in the interests of the health, safety, and morals of its citizens, need not be included under the "full faith and credit" clause. A state may also make use of its "police powers" to insist that doctors, teachers, and other professional or skilled workers obtain new state licenses. Thus, a state may refuse to recognize a driver's license obtained in another state if it believes this is necessary for the safety of its other citizens. Also, states may impose different requirements for obtaining a legal divorce.

The powers of Congress are found in Article I, Section 8. Because they are specifically listed in the Constitution, they are referred to as delegated, expressed, or enumerated powers. However, Article I, Section 8 also concludes with a clause that allows Congress to make all laws that are "necessary and proper" (see page 26) to enable the federal government to do what it must to govern the nation effectively. While this clause grants no new powers, the framers of the Constitution believed that it gave the federal government the authority to deal with circumstances not contemplated by them.

Because the states existed before the nation, the framers of the Constitution understood very well that the states could not be expected to give up all of their powers to a central authority. If you turn to the diagram (see Appendix) you will see, in simplified form, the provisions made in the Constitution for power-sharing between the states and the federal government.

The history of government in America may be thought of as a tug-of-war between those who favor limiting the powers of Congress to only those listed in the Constitution, and those who take the broader view that implied in the Constitution is the authority to do what needs to be done to meet new conditions. The United States Supreme Court often intervenes to determine whether or not either Congress or the states have gone too far.

Because the powers of Congress are enumerated in the Constitution, it is sometimes said to be a government of limited powers. On the other hand, no comparable list of state powers can be found in the

Constitution. Instead, its framers assumed that powers not given to Congress are reserved to the states. The powers of the states are described as reserved, or residual, powers. This principle was confirmed in Amendment X in the Bill of Rights, which states, "The powers not delegated to the United States by the Constitution nor prohibited by it to the states are reserved to the states respectively or to the people."

As you can see from the diagram (see Appendix), the federal government has enumerated powers. State governments have the remaining (residual) powers provided that they are not prohibited by the Constitution. Some powers are concurrent (at the same time) in nature: the states and the federal government share them. While states may not make treaties or coin money, both can set qualifications for voting. Both the states and the federal government may impose taxes. The framers of the Constitution provided for a federal system in which the federal government was supreme; nevertheless, the governing authority for those issues over which the people had immediate concern was left to the states.

In order to assure the states that their powers would not be unduly eroded, James Madison in *The Federalist* article No. 39 pointed out that each state would send two members to a powerful United States Senate and representatives, the number based on the size of its population, to the House of Representatives. "The House of Representatives," Madison explained, "will derive its powers from the people of America; . . . The Senate, on the other hand, will derive its powers from the States, as political and coequal societies. . . ."[1] Over the years, state and federal authority clashed, and at times some states refused to carry out the laws imposed by the federal government or even threatened to leave the Union.

The most extreme case of the exercise of states'

rights occurred over the question of slavery; this led to the Civil War. The outcome of this war was that slavery was forever and everywhere abolished and the Union was confirmed as indissoluble. By interpreting the provisions of Amendment XIV, which was among the post-Civil War amendments, the United States Supreme Court, in a number of decisions since 1925, held that the Bill of Rights was binding upon the states as well as upon the federal government.

The federal system provided by the framers of the Constitution was a unique contribution to the art of government. While it has many advantages, it also has many disadvantages. Among the advantages of a federal system of government are the following:

1. A federal system, in which states are vested with considerable authority, allows for a government "close to the people" and so may help protect liberty and encourage republican principles.

2. By having government entities smaller and less remote from the people than the national government, greater participation by the people themselves is encouraged.

3. Through state governments, greater diversity is possible and regional differences and cultural values can be taken into account when legislating on behalf of the state. Such diversity encourages experimentation in new forms of government and administrative efficiency. In his famous decision in *New State Ice Company v. Liebmann* (1932), Justice Louis D. Brandeis argued that "a single courageous state may, if its citizens choose, serve as a laboratory, and try novel social and economic experiments without risk to the rest of the country."

Women, for example, were given the right to vote in the territory of Wyoming in 1869, long before Amendment XIX (1920), which extended the right to vote to women nationally. In 1889, Massachusetts adopted the secret ballot for all state elections. Minimum wage laws, pollution control programs, and the regulation of labor for women and children were first experiments of state governments.

Some states have adopted the provision for an initiative—the initiating of legislation or a constitutional amendment by petitions of the citizens. Other states have adopted recall—the removal by the citizens of elected officials before the expiration of their term. (Alaska, Arizona, California, Colorado, Idaho, Kansas, Louisiana, Michigan, Nevada, North Dakota, Oregon, Washington, and Wisconsin are states with provision for recall.) The State of Oregon adopted innovative plans in 1993 to ration medical care among the poor and uninsured. The aim was to give medical services to patients with the greatest possibility of a successful outcome. Under President Clinton, portions of Oregon's proposal may become a part of his national health care reform, an example of how experiments in state governments may influence national policy.

4. The founders were fearful that the national government might become both too powerful and inefficient. They thought that state governments, as smaller units, would improve administrative efficiency and provide opportunities for more detailed study of important legislation. States were expected to share the burden of government by reducing the amount of work required at the national level. James Madison was so convinced of the need for state governments that he insisted in *The Federalist* No. 14, that even if the states were initially abolished it would be in the national interest to reinstate them. "Were it proposed," he wrote, ". . . to abolish the governments of the particular States . . . it would not be difficult to show that if they were abolished the general government would be compelled, by the principle of self-preservation, to reinstate them. . . ."[2]

5. Conflicts may be more easily resolved at state and local levels: for example, decisions on salaries and workloads for teachers or firefighters, choice of school textbooks, which areas of a community may be suitable for businesses or for high-rise apartments.

6. Showing great insight, the framers of the Constitution were aware that before long new territories would want to enter the Union as states. These new geographic regions would have economies, life-styles, and interests possibly different from those of the states on the eastern seaboard. Through a federal system, new states could be admitted on a basis equal to those of the original states.

Despite these real advantages, a federal system of government has a number of disadvantages, which can be summarized as follows.

1. While diversity may be desirable, it also creates inequities. Thus, penalties for crimes vary considerably throughout the nation. In some states a person convicted of murder will be executed. In other states capital punishment is prohibited. In some states youths as young as ten may be tried as adults for certain crimes while in other states they may not be tried as adults until they are eighteen.

2. With different layers of government tensions develop. Is the state or the federal government responsible for passing legislation or administering a program? Often, duplication of responsibility results. For example, both state and federal government can seek to monitor labeling of food packages or to determine sanitation, health, and safety standards in the workplace. With duplication comes a lack of accountability. Who is responsible when a citizen is harmed by inappropriate legislation or inept administration? Since an increasingly large number of programs require what are essentially federal-state partnerships, lack of accountability and costly duplication of effort may result.

3. States vary widely in size, resources, and the wealth they can generate. Federalism may not adequately differentiate between rich and poor states. Children going to school in poor states may be taught in inferior facilities, sit in larger classes, use outworn textbooks, and have fewer amenities. Children in rich states may have the use of a lunch room, a swimming pool, superior athletic facilities, smaller classes, and more educational technology in the form of computerized and televised instruction. Moreover, disparities in wealth create differences in levels of medical care and welfare to which residents may be entitled. Because of such disparities the quality of life, opportunities to enjoy a higher standard of living, and even the length of life itself may result from accidents of geography.

4. Because state governments are smaller than the federal government, they may be more subject to intimidation by powerful special interests. And while corruption and scandal have by no means been absent on the federal level, it is at the state and local levels of government that corruption has been most evident in America. Political bossism, kickbacks to gain favorable treatment in matters of taxation, a single newspaper dependent for its sustenance on a single interest group—all serve to make local and state governments less effective than the Founding Fathers expected them to be. Remember that the practice of using slave labor persisted because some states protected the institution of slavery. And it was at the state level that discrimination in housing, voting, transportation, and schooling was most widespread. James Bryce, the distinguished nineteenth-century British political scientist, was highly critical of local government in America. "The one conspicuous failure of the United States," he called it.[3]

5. Some political scientists insist that federalism is only a myth, and that in reality the federal government has by far the greater clout. They go on to say that states have, during the more than 200 years since the Constitution was written, lost so much power that they are now servants of the federal government. This is especially true because the federal government has a greater ability to raise money through taxes and to make funds available to the states only if certain requirements are met, for example, the building of roads and bridges, providing medical care, distributing welfare benefits, and so on.

Walt Whitman (1819–1892), the American poet, expressed the chronic American suspicion of excessive federal authority. In *Leaves of Grass* he applauded what could be called the "federal creed":

> *"To The States, or any one of them, or any city of*
> *The States,*
> *Resist much, obey little;*
> *Once unquestioning obedience, once fully enslaved;*
> *no nation, state, city, of this earth, ever afterward resumes its liberty.*

Whitman's "federal creed" notwithstanding, federalism has meant different things at different times. To the authors of *The Federalist* federalism meant that the central government would exercise greater authority. Their dissatisfaction with the government under the Articles of Confederation had brought them to Philadelphia in the first place. Their problem was how to centralize authority in the national government without destroying the preexisting states.

Federalism has meant states rights, a strict construction of the Constitution, to more recent administrations, especially the Republican administrations of presidents Dwight Eisenhower (1953–1961), Richard Nixon (1969–1974), Ronald Reagan (1981–1989), and George Bush (1989–1993). The return of power to the states resonates well among the American people in that it implies a national government free of a "bloated" bureaucracy, a return to simpler times, and a more responsive government. Because the Constitution stacks the cards against the states, the federal government has usually had the upper hand. As a result, the power of the national government in Washington, D.C., keeps growing. Let us see why it does.

In Philadelphia during that long, hot summer in 1787, the framers of the Constitution took a break from their work to stroll along the Delaware River, where John Fitch was demonstrating a revolutionary new mode of transportation—the steamboat. This distinguished group could not know how much technology would, in the future, call into question their finely honed federal system. Sojourns in space, travel to the moon, global instantaneous telecommunications, all demonstrate the pivotal role of the national government.

Government could not be small even if it wanted to given the growth of giant industries and the national labor unions. The need to restore equity among the states, to correct widespread racial discrimination, to extend freedom of religion and freedom of expression to all the people of all the states, necessitates an expanded government. "There is a peculiar futility in inveighing against only one of the leviathans (giants) of American life—that of government—without recognizing that it has come into being to balance the other leviathans."[4] Liberals and conservatives, Republicans and Democrats, Northerners and Southerners have, without regard for consistency, raised the cry of "states rights." Yet the fact remains that the federal government was intended to be the senior partner in the federal system, and it has not only remained so but has strengthened its grip as well.

Centralization has increased because many problems now cross state lines. The air in New York will remain polluted unless New Jersey controls the emissions from its oil refineries. The Great Lakes will be unfit for fish or wildlife unless the states bordering them cooperate in cleaning them up. Education cannot be more effective if even one state maintains a substandard school system. If some states are more generous with their welfare payments, the poor will move there and place an undue burden upon these states. It now takes a federal effort to keep crime under control. Drugs have become so widespread that enforcement of laws against illicit drugs can no longer be left entirely to the states, and a "war" against drugs under a federal drug czar becomes essential. An infectious disease such as Acquired Immune Deficiency Syndrome (AIDS) cannot be combatted adequately through state efforts alone.

On January 1, 1993, the European nations formed a common market known as the European Economic Area. It will become the world's largest trading bloc and the United States will, economically, no longer be the world's greatest market. At a time when Western Europe is uniting economically, Eastern Europe is fragmenting. The former Soviet Union becomes the Commonwealth of Independent States and Yugoslavia is violently torn into several hostile nations. In their magnitude and implications these changes are not unlike those that were unfolding when the framers wrote the Constitution of the United States. They could not predict a French Revolution and the overthrow of monarchy; nevertheless they were aware of the meaning of unfolding events to a fledgling nation.

The nation is today faced with foreign crises to which only the national government can respond. Can the nation remain strong centrally without destroying the republican form of government that the Constitution provides? Essentially, the issue for our time may be succinctly stated, "Can we be centralized and democratic at the same time?"

Government in the United States does not only consist of the federal and state governments, but includes many other forms of government as well. This aggravates the problem. The impact of these governments on how America is governed is our next concern.

During the first half of the nineteenth century, the federal system was described accurately as a layer cake. The first layer of government, concerned mainly with the national economy, defense, currency, interstate commerce, and foreign affairs, was the government in Washington, D.C. The second layer of government, that of the states, was concerned mainly with local problems of the health, safety, welfare, and education of its citizens.

The framers of the Constitution anticipated that as the nation grew, additional states would seek to join the American federation. What they could not anticipate was the multiplicity of local governments on the one hand, and the vast expansion of federal power on the other. As a result, the metaphor that best describes government in America is that of a marble cake rather than a layer cake. Morton Grodzins, who coined the metaphor, recognized that in modern times the American is not only a citizen of the nation and of the state, but is also a citizen of a host of other local governments.[5]

According to the *Statistical Abstract of the United States*, there are 83,237 different local governments—counties, municipalities, townships, school districts, and numerous kinds of special districts. "As defined by the census, governmental units include all agencies or bodies having an organized existence, government character, and substantial autonomy."[6] As a result, Morton Grodzins reminds us, there is no neat division into federal and state functions. Instead, "If one looks closely, it appears that virtually all governments are involved in virtually all functions. . . . Functions of American governments are shared."[7]

In May 1992, when violence erupted in Los Angeles, the local authorities were unable to restore order. When, in the same year, Hurricane Andrew devastated southern Florida, it took a federal effort to provide relief to the citizens. In these crises, the theory cherished by the Founding Fathers, that state governments would perform those functions that were closest to the people, reflected reality less and less.

Contrary to the beliefs of the Founding Fathers, the federal government touches the lives of everyone directly. The most obvious example is the United States Postal System, upon which we rely for our daily mail. Federal milk subsidies and federal aid to school lunch programs determine what will be served in the school cafeterias. Many American farmers look to the federal government, not to the states, for farm subsidies (financial help). In rural areas of the country, it is often the federal and not the state or local government that is closest to the people.

How does one account for the rich mosaic of America's federalism? The answer, in part, is that a state's problems do not stop at its borders. An aerial view of the United States reveals the arbitrary way in which the borders of many of the western states were drawn. The geometric, checkerboard shapes suggest that states such as Colorado, Utah, and Wyoming need regional institutions to deal with their problems of clean air and potable (drinkable) water. The toxic waters of the Great Lakes, for example, could not have been subjected to pollution containment and control without the regional cooperation of the bordering states. Transportation would be far more chaotic between New Jersey and New York without the formation of the Port of New York Authority, which controls highways, tunnels, bridges, and airports serving the area. The combined effort of several states, under federal direction, is required if dealers in illicit drugs are to be brought to justice.

Moreover, most Americans live in environments the Census Bureau describes as Metropolitan Statistical Areas (MSA). These areas often extend across state lines, as for example, in New York, northern

New Jersey, Long Island, and parts of Connecticut. The cities of Philadelphia, Pennsylvania; Wilmington, Delaware; and Trenton, New Jersey; form another MSA. In the United States 77.5 percent of the population lives in metropolitan areas. It is in these areas that 90 percent of the nation's growth takes place. Consequently, regional approaches to problems become indispensable, and the centralization of government in federal hands is further encouraged.

States have increasingly looked to the federal government for financial aid to its poor. States do not have access to the revenue sources available to the federal government. As a result, states increasingly administer the federal allocations and look to the federal government for guidance in setting minimum standards. However, the administrations of Presidents Reagan and Bush attempted to "get government off the backs of the people"—that is, the states were required to assume greater responsibility for public services.

Revenues to pay for those services shifted to the states were not always forthcoming. As a result, in the early 1990s states found themselves overwhelmed with the need to provide services to the homeless, for example, without adequate finances to do so. As the depression of those years deepened, states found themselves increasingly hard-pressed and shifted funds from one activity (police protection or education) to another (hospitals and welfare) in a vain effort to make limited resources go farther.

Despite efforts by many presidents, especially by President Reagan, to limit the responsibilities of the federal government, growth persists. In itself, such growth is neither good nor bad, simply inevitable. ". . . it is futile to try to limit government to some defined sphere. Nothing of importance can be done to stop the spread of federal power, let alone to restore something like the division of powers agreed upon by the framers of the Constitution."[8] But if the intent of the framers of the Constitution cannot be implemented because of unforeseen developments, does the Constitution require revision to reflect more accurately how America is actually governed?

If states need the federal government for the finances to address their residents' problems, is there a danger that states are inviting "Big Brother" to tell them what, when, where, and how to do it? Is such "Big Brotherism" a threat to democracy and to the states themselves? With the proliferation of government, do problems that seem to be common to all become the responsibility of no one, and are they treated only as symptoms, with the underlying causes going unaddressed? Because the bone of contention is sometimes in one place (the federal government) and sometimes in another (state government), some insist that the federal system has become a system of buck-passing. Complex and controversial issues are not resolved but remain in what President Franklin D. Roosevelt once called a "no man's land" between federal, state, and local governments.

In 1982, centralization of authority in the federal government was still seen as the dominant trend. Yet John Naisbitt in his popular book *Megatrends*, written in 1982, noted a contrary tendency in many areas toward decentralization. He wrote, ". . . the ability to get things done—has shifted away from Congress and the presidency to the states, cities, towns, and neighborhoods."[9] He insisted that the old "top down" philosophy was rapidly eroding and was being supplanted by a "bottoms up" philosophy in which smaller units of government would transform America. Mr. Naisbitt identified areas in which states have exercised a "new assertiveness":

- *San Diego, California, constructed a streetcar system entirely without federal money.*

- *Ohio, Michigan, Illinois, Indiana, Kentucky, Pennsylvania, and West Virginia have plans for a high-speed train based on Japanese and West German technology to compete with Amtrack.*
- *New Jersey, Delaware, and Pennsylvania tightened regulations with regard to the dumping of radioactive waste.[10] Former Governor of Colorado, Richard Lamm declared, "The day of the state has come and gone—and come back again."[11]*

But are these "megatrends" premature? The railroad that Ohio and the other states are planning has yet to be built. While the states can improve the environment, they cannot go far without federal encouragement. A specialist on the federal system prefers to say: "At the beginning of its third century, the condition of American federalism is best characterized as ambiguous but promising. This, in itself, represents a great advance for noncentralized government over the situation that prevailed between 1965 and 1980, during which the trend was rather unambiguously centralizing."[12]

Because centralizing and decentralizing forces are concurrently at work, the future of federalism remains unclear. The federal government continues to have the upper hand in national/state relations. The states appear to be establishing a new assertiveness in their relationships with the federal government. But they can do so only if they work together with other states in trying to solve related problems. Perhaps in the third century just ahead, federalism will not disappear, but will take new and perhaps as yet unidentified but vigorous forms.

If important changes in the federal structure can be anticipated for the next century, can parallel changes be required in that other pillar of American government, separation of powers? In the next chapter, we shall explore this question.

44

CHECKS AND BALANCES: SAFEGUARD OF DEMOCRACY OR FORMULA FOR STALEMATE?

The Congress was the pride of the framers of the United States Constitution. Today, Americans take little pride in their legislative body. In a *New York Times/CBS News* poll in April 1992, 75 percent of those polled disapproved of the way Congress was handling its job.[1] In 1992, bounced checks drawn on the congressional bank especially set up to serve members of Congress triggered the citizens' outcry against a "do-nothing" Congress.

Ninety-six percent of Congress members remain in office term after term. As a result, they make arrangements to assure themselves of reelection, to improve their salaries, and to obtain perks. Special parking privileges, inexpensive haircuts and medical care, low-priced meals, free postage to constituents, and inexpensive athletic facilities are only a few of such privileges. The discovery of these expensive fringe benefits increased the anger of people and raised questions about the integrity of members of Congress.

Although the framers of the Constitution took considerable pride in the legislative body they had established, they were afraid that it could exercise tyranny unless powers were distributed among other institutions of government. To prevent tyranny, they created three distinct branches of the national government. Separation of powers, as this is called, is central to the government established by the Constitution. How separation of powers was intended to work, how it does work, and why it doesn't work as well as it should, as well as what can be done about it, are the subject of this chapter.

Thomas Jefferson objected to many features of the new Constitution. Upon his return from France, he voiced his opposition to a legislature of two houses. At a breakfast with George Washington, he asked why a two-house legislature was needed. Washington countered by asking why Jefferson poured his coffee from cup to saucer. "To cool it," Jefferson replied.

"Even so," said Washington, "we pour legislation into the senatorial saucer to cool it."

With this remark, Washington summed up the intention of the Founding Fathers in creating the two houses of Congress. Article I, Section 1, of the Constitution declares, "all legislative powers . . . shall be vested in a Congress of the United States which shall consist of a Senate and House of Representatives."

While federalism is the division of authority between the national government and the states, separation of powers is the authority given to branches of the national government to perform different functions. According to the principle of separation of powers, the federal government consists of three separate branches, each with a different set of duties.

Congress has the power to make laws.
The president has the power to enforce the laws.
The courts have the power to interpret the laws.

By establishing three separate branches of government, the Founding Fathers set up a system in which one branch of government could prevent the other two branches from exercising tyrannical power. The procedures involved in passing laws for the nation further illustrate the principle of separation of powers:

1. *It takes both houses of Congress, the Senate, or upper house, and the House of Representatives, or lower house, to pass a bill.*

2. *A bill becomes a law only when it is signed by the president.*

3. *The president may refuse to sign (veto) a bill passed by both houses of Congress.*

4. *Congress may, by a two-third majority in each House, pass a bill over the president's veto.*

5. *The Supreme Court may declare a law passed by Congress and signed by the president unconstitutional, if a case involving the law is brought before it.*

6. *Treaties negotiated by the president with foreign countries must have the approval of two-thirds of the Senate.*

7. *The president may call Congress into a special session if he/she believes it is necessary.*

Drawing on their experiences with many of the state constitutions that provided for separation of powers, the framers of the Constitution sought, above all else, "a government of laws and not of men." "If men were angels," Madison explained, "no government would be necessary. If angels were to govern men, neither internal nor external controls on government would be necessary. You must first," Madison continued, "enable the government to control the governed; and in the next place oblige it to control itself."[2]

Separation of powers is not essential for democracy. Britain is a constitutional monarchy and parliamentary democracy, but separation of powers does not exist. As long as the British Prime Minister's political party has a majority in the House of Commons, the Prime Minister's power is complete. The essential obstacle to tyrannical rule by the Prime Minister and the majority party is their fear of not being reelected. Unlike the Congress, the British House of Commons can do anything it wishes—there is no separation of powers and no system of checks and balances to limit its authority. However, a system of separation of powers does not by itself prevent arbitrary government. The framers of the Constitution therefore built in a system of checks and balances that would enforce separation of duties and put a brake on arbitrary exercise of legislative, executive, or judicial authority.

CHECKS AND BALANCES

If separation of powers is an overarching principle of the framework of government in the United States, checks and balances may be thought of as the means by which the writers of the Constitution ensured that the three branches of government would keep an eye on one another. So that one branch of government might check on each of the others, legislative, executive, and judicial branches are assigned different duties. To ensure that the branches of government remain forever separate, the framers of the Constitution also provided that: (1) the executive, legislative, and judicial branches would be chosen in different ways; (2) there would be different qualifications for office; and (3) office terms would be for different periods of time.

As provided in the Constitution, originally the members of the House of Representatives would serve a two-year term, and were the only officials directly elected by the voters. For the United States Senate, the legislature of each state was to choose two senators to serve for a term of six years. Moreover, to insure stability, the term of the senators was staggered so that one-third of the Senate was to be chosen every two years. However, on May 31, 1913, the United States Constitution was amended (Amendment XVII) to provide for the direct election of senators. Today, both senators and representatives are directly chosen by the voters of their states.

The president serves for four years and may be reelected. George Washington set a precedent of presidents holding office for no more than two terms. However, Franklin D. Roosevelt, president from 1933 to 1945, was reelected three times. Amendment XXII, adopted in 1951, limits modern presidents to only two terms. The framers of the Constitution intended the president to be chosen by electors and not directly by the people.

Judges of the Supreme Court hold office for life, and are appointed by the president with the advice and consent of the Senate. Members of the president's cabinet are also appointed by the president with the advice and consent of the Senate but serve at the president's pleasure.

Additional checks and balances are provided in the Constitution. According to Article I, Section 6, no member of Congress may hold another federal office at the same time, and no federal officeholder may at the same time be a member of Congress. The process of amending the Constitution (see p. 99) may check the power of the Supreme Court to interpret the law. In extreme cases, the president may be impeached, that is, brought to trial by Congress. The House brings the charges, the Senate acts as jury, and the chief justice of the Supreme Court presides.

The framers of the Constitution sought to insure that each branch of government would be checked by either or both of the others by creating different requirements for each branch. For example, to serve in the House of Representatives, a person must be at least twenty-five years old, a citizen of the United States for seven years, and a resident, at the time of election, of the state from which he or she is chosen. A candidate for the Senate must be at least thirty years old, a citizen of the United States for nine years, and at the time of election, a resident of the state from which he or she is chosen. The president of the United States must be at least thirty-five years of age, a resident of the United States for at least fourteen years and must be a citizen of the United States by birth, not by naturalization. Thus, those born abroad who later become citizens are not eligible for the presidency. There are no age or citizenship requirements for members of the Supreme Court.

DOES SEPARATION OF POWERS STILL WORK? In a letter to George Washington in 1788, John Jay wrote: "Government without liberty is a curse; but on the other hand, liberty without government is far from being a blessing."[3] While the framers of the Constitution sought to provide the blessings of liberty they also wanted a government that worked. In attempting to solve the conflict between too much government and too much liberty, they relied on a combination of separation of powers and checks and balances. However, after two hundred years of the experiment in republicanism and democracy that has largely worked, concerns are increasing that separation of powers may be the source of mounting dissatisfaction with government. Let us examine a number of shortcomings with separation of powers that have been identified.

1. The political scientist, James Q. Wilson, writes: "There are two fundamental arguments for a constitutional system of separate institutions sharing power. It helps preserve liberty and it slows the pace of political change."[4] The price of preserving liberty, however, may include the cost of a pace of political change

too slow to be responsive to the nation's needs in tumultuous times. When does healthy tension between a president and Congress become a standoff, causing problems to go unattended?

2. Because separation of powers slows the pace of political change and government responsiveness, in times of crisis the president tends to exercise leadership. For example, Thomas Jefferson exploited the opportunity in 1803 to purchase the Louisiana Territory thereby doubling the size of the nation. Abraham Lincoln led the nation through the crisis of the Civil war, and Franklin D. Roosevelt guided the nation through the severe depression of the 1930s and the Second World War.

3. By establishing a system of separation of powers and reenforcing it with a system of checks and balances, the framers of the Constitution deliberately encouraged inefficiency in government. Just as the federal system encourages buck-passing between the central government and state governments, so buck-passing is encouraged between Congress and the president.

4. Many members of Congress or the president perceive that the way to reelection and higher office is to avoid taking courageous positions on controversial issues or serious problems. Consequently, there is a tendency to delay, postpone, ignore, or otherwise dillydally before acting. Only when Congress is forced to act, does it do so. Often, by then, the legislation, however well conceived is both too little and too late to correct the problem. In 1992, it took a disastrous riot in Los Angeles to awaken both the Congress and the president to the need to improve inner cities. It had taken a riot to awaken those in positions of power, and when they acted, they did so timidly. The legislation to bring some long-term relief to Los Angeles was vetoed by President Bush.

5. Perhaps the most serious problem with separation of powers is that it was developed for a republican form of government. The framers of the Constitution were concerned about the tyranny exercised by the masses of common people. They did not want to see a government ruled by King Mob, and they did not wish to experience another Shays's Rebellion (see p. 19). Separation of powers was a way of assuring that the masses could not exercise tyranny over the propertied classes. Few, if any, would argue for abandoning separation of powers, because we now have a democracy as well as a republic. However, those who wish to change the Constitution or go so far as to draft a new one, propose different ways of separating powers to make government responsive to the will of the people. (For more on this subject see chapter 6.)

6. A perennial debate among scholars of the American Constitution concerns the intention of the framers to give the Supreme Court the power of judicial review. In the famous case of *Marbury v. Madison* (1803), Chief Justice John Marshall boldly asserted that it was "the province and duty of the judicial department to say what the law is. . . ." Through this decision the Court could rule on the extent, powers, and functions of the other branches. In the prolonged skirmishing between the president and the Congress—the executive and legislative branches—the Supreme Court may act as referee when a case is brought to it and try to resolve disputes based on its interpretation of the Constitution. Most likely the Supreme Court has, over two centuries, acquired powers vastly greater than intended by the framers of the Constitution.

7. Similarly, while the Constitution gave the president a generous amount of authority, most of the presidential authority has been accumulated through precedent and tradition. Strong presidents, in the absence of restraint from other branches, did what they thought necessary as chief executives. In making appointments and in negotiating treaties with foreign powers, the president must seek the "advice and consent" of the Senate.

THE CONSTITUTIONAL BATTLE OF THE CENTURIES

Separation of powers is a prime target of those who want to change the Constitution. Dissatisfaction with separation of powers arises largely out of the battles between Congress and the president. For two hundred years the "battle of the centuries" has raged, with first one side and then the other gaining the advantage.

A number of examples of these battles during the post-World War II years follow:

- *In 1952, during the war with North Korea, President Harry S. Truman took over the steel industry which was threatened with a labor strike, to avoid a national catastrophe. However, the Supreme Court ruled in the case of* Youngstown Sheet and Tube Co. v. Sawyer, *that President Truman had gone too far. The Court held that he could act as he did only if (1) congressional authorization had been obtained; or (2) specific power to do so could be found in the Constitution. Since neither could be found, the Court held that Truman had acted unconstitutionally and refused to support his action.*
- *In 1974, President Richard Nixon sought to avoid surrendering his tapes of his conversations in the infamous Watergate scandal. Nixon refused the subpoenas (summons) of Congress by citing the separation of powers. In the case of* The United States v. Nixon, *the Court rejected his arguments and insisted that he respond to the congressional demands.*
- *In 1983, the Supreme Court reprimanded Congress for exceeding its authority by exercising the "legislative veto." Between 1932 and 1982, Congress had delegated authority to a number of regulatory commissions, but retained the right to veto a regulation it disliked. In* Immigration and Naturalization Service v. Chadha, *the Court held that once Congress gave the executive branch authority to issue regulations, "it must abide by its delegation of authority until that delegation is legislatively altered or revoked." And in response to the claim of Congress that the legislative veto was necessary to resolve conflicts between the executive and the legislative branches of government, the Court*

declared, "Convenience and efficiency are not the primary objectives—or the hallmarks—of democratic government. . . ."

- *In 1986, the United States Supreme Court struck down important features of the Gramm-Rudman-Hollings law which attempted to reduce the federal budget. The law gave the comptroller general, the head of the General Accounting Office, the authority to ratify the amount and scope of federal budget cuts, which the president would have to follow. In* Bowsher v. Synar *the Court declared this unconstitutional because the General Accounting Office was a part of the legislative branch and so lacked the authority to bind the president.[5] On domestic matters there is a standoff between Congress and the president.*

Not so, however, in the area of foreign policy where conflict between Congress and the president is likely to be resolved in favor of the president. In *United States v. Curtiss Wright Export Company* (1936) the Court held, "the president alone has the power to speak or listen as a representative of the nation." While inroads have been made on the president's authority, nevertheless, deference for presidential prerogative is shown in foreign affairs.

While the constitutional "battle of the centuries" between president and Congress has prevented tyranny, it has also often thwarted prompt action. A number of changes have been necessary in the course of two hundred years to moderate the constitutional conflict.

MODIFICATIONS IN SEPARATION OF POWERS If the principle of separation of powers had been strictly observed, America would have been ungovernable. Fortunately, modifications of the principle have taken place.

MODIFICATIONS BY FORMAL AMENDMENT:
Amendment XVII requires the direct election of United States Senators by citizens rather than selection by legislatures in their respective states. The framers of the Constitution intended that the members of the House and Senate be chosen in different ways to make it possible for one house of Congress to "check" and "balance" the other. Today that principle has been breached in the interests of greater democracy, thus all members of Congress are now elected directly by the people.

MODIFICATIONS BY CHANGED
ELECTION PROCEDURES:
When the Constitution was written, its framers foolishly assumed that political parties would not develop and that the common people could not be trusted. The framers sought to insulate the choice of the president from both party and people. Toward this end they established a body of electors, the Electoral College, made up of wise people equal to the number of representatives and senators to which each state is entitled. Chosen by the legislatures of the states, or in any manner the states determined, the electors would exercise independent judgment and choose the best persons to be president and vice president.

This system of choosing the president never worked in the way the framers of the Constitution intended. While the electoral college still exists, its members are not chosen by state legislatures nor are they necessarily men and women of great wisdom. Instead, they are usually people of some local prominence who are chosen by their political parties. In choosing the president, the electors make no independent judgment but are pledged to vote for the presidential candidate who receives a majority of the votes in their state. (According to Amendment XXIII,

Washington, D.C. was assigned three electors. Thus the electoral college is made up of 438 people and 270 votes are needed to elect the president.) These changes were not made by law. Instead, they are part of the "unwritten constitution" established through custom and tradition. Moreover, some believe that further changes are needed in the way the president is elected and that these changes should be authorized through legislation or amendment. (See chapter 6.)

MODIFICATIONS BY POLITICAL PARTIES:
The framers of the Constitution sought to eliminate the destructive influence of "factions" or political parties. Ironically, in the very arguments over the ratification of the Constitution, (see p. 22) two political parties were formed. The Federalists urged the adoption of the Constitution while the Anti-Federalists feared that the Constitution had given too much power to the central government. The development of political parties has made separation of powers possible in that in the political area some, but by no means all, of the conflicts caused by separation of powers may be resolved.

MODIFICATIONS BY CREATING
A FOURTH BRANCH OF GOVERNMENT:
Congress itself may have modified the original concept of separation of powers by delegating powers to the president and independent regulatory commissions such as the Federal Aviation Administration, Interstate Commerce Commission, Food and Drug Administration, Federal Communications Commission, and Environmental Protection Agency, to cite but a few examples. As a "fourth branch" of government, these agencies are technically under the president who, for the most part, appoints its members

for definite terms with the approval of the Senate. The president has the authority, granted by Congress, to remove the commission chairperson and with this power the president wields considerable influence on the management and decisions of the agency.

These regulatory agencies have quasi-legislative, executive, or judicial functions. However, these agencies have become so widespread that in many areas of government the principle of separation of powers has been drastically modified. The principle of separation of powers was at least partially restored when the Supreme Court invalidated the use of the legislative veto (See p. 53).

MODIFICATIONS THROUGH
THE WAR POWERS RESOLUTION:
An area of potential conflict between Congress and the president is war powers. As a safeguard against a president who may use such a power indiscriminately, Article I, Section 8 of the Constitution gives to the Congress, not the president, the power to declare war. Yet, Congress has never declared war except at the request of the president. The Supreme Court has upheld the right of Congress to draft soldiers, ration food and gasoline, regulate production, and distribute raw materials. It has even upheld the right of Congress to relocate Japanese-Americans who were moved from their homes to internment camps during World War II, a grave violation of their civil liberties.

However, according to the Constitution, the president is commander in chief of the armed forces. From this authority comes the power of the president to wage war. While Congress can declare war, only the president can muster the troops to fight it. Because of the president's authority as commander in chief, the president can send troops to areas in which American lives or interests may be endangered. Thus, without a declaration of war, presidents intervened militarily in Panama in 1903, in Russia and Mexico in 1917, in Korea in 1950, and in Lebanon in 1952. It was without a declaration of war that 543,400 troops were sent to Vietnam between 1964 and 1969.

Primarily because of the national fear of another Vietnam, Congress in 1973 passed the War Powers Resolution, over President Nixon's veto. The measure was designed to limit the ability of the president to make war. According to its provisions, Congress and the president were to consult "in every possible instance" and to make sure that "the collective judgment" of the president and Congress would be relied upon before troops are sent into battle. However, the provisions of the resolution are ambiguous and are difficult to interpret and to carry out.

In spite of the War Powers Resolution, President Carter sent troops to Iran in 1980 to free the American hostages. In 1983 President Reagan sent troops to Granada ostensibly to rescue American students and other United States citizens but also to diminish a perceived Communist threat to the island. In 1989, President Bush sent troops to Panama to capture General Manuel Noriega. In the case of the Gulf War with Iraq (Desert Storm), while Congress did not declare war, it did reluctantly give President Bush authorization to use American armed forces to expel Iraqi troops from Kuwait.

In an area as vital as the security of the nation, the power of Congress to "declare war" and the president's power to "wage war" continue to clash. The constitutionality of the War Powers Resolution has not been fully resolved, nor has the cooperation between Congress and the president during a national emergency been worked out. Nevertheless, the powers of the president to wage war have been partially dimin-

58

ished by the War Powers Resolution. Has this made it more difficult for the president to act in an emergency? In extraordinary situations it is the obligation of the president to act even without explicit authorization from either Congress or the Constitution. This ambiguity is inherent in separation of powers.

If American government is to function effectively, the president and the Congress must work together. But what if strong personalities in both branches clash over partisan politics, specific issues, foreign and domestic circumstances, and bring government to a standstill?

DIVIDED GOVERNMENT

When Congress and the president are from the same party some degree of harmony and cooperation may be expected. Because such harmony existed during Woodrow Wilson's first term as president (1913–1917) his legislative agenda, which he called the New Freedom, could be adopted. Between 1933 and 1936, because Congress and the president were of one party, Franklin D. Roosevelt could get enacted his New Deal program to combat the depression. And between 1963 and 1965, President Lyndon Johnson could see his Great Society war on poverty adopted by Congress.

Even when Congress and the president are of the same party, however, harmony does not necessarily follow. And when the president and the Congress are of different parties, a stalemate does not necessarily result. During the early years of President Reagan's administration, a Republican Senate and a Democratic House of Representatives, in which conservative Democrats worked with Republicans, enacted important tax and spending cuts. Some measure of cooperation between the legislature and the executive branch was temporarily achieved because Ronald Reagan was effective in going over the head of Con-

59

gress and communicating directly with the American people.

Between 1947 and 1992, the overwhelming majority of the Congresses has been controlled by parties in opposition to the president. As a result, divided government has been characteristic of the post-World War II years. While some fear that a stalemate in government may endanger the nation because of friction between a majority in Congress of one party and a president of another, at least one scholar has insisted that, ". . . unified as opposed to divided control has not made an important difference in recent times. . . . Important laws have materialized at a rate largely unrelated to conditions of party control."[6] Nevertheless, because of the fear that gridlock in government may result, there have been calls for modifying separation of powers or for eliminating it altogether. What reforms are proposed will be considered in chapter 6.

Because the American government seems to function in fits and starts, the historian Arthur Schlesinger Jr., referred to this tendency as "cycles of history." In some cycles, a stalemate seems to be imminent. In others, great leaps for the better appear to be made. It has fallen to the nation's political parties to mediate these cycles of history. How effectively have parties served the needs of American government?

OUR POLITICAL PARTIES: AN ENDANGERED SPECIES?

The function of political parties in America is to elect their candidates to local and national office. Everything else political parties do—and they do many things—is subordinate to this purpose. That this function is being poorly performed is evident in the alienation (dissatisfaction) of many American voters. For too many, the political process does not seem important to their lives.

Evidence of the electorate's dissatisfaction is mounting. Warren Miller, a political scientist from the University of Arizona, found that voter participation declined roughly from 65 percent in 1960 to 50 percent in 1988.[1] In the midterm elections of 1990 the Committee for the Study of the American Electorate found that only 36 percent of the 106 million eligible voters bothered to cast their ballot.[2]

Although nonvoters tend to be less prosperous, less educated, and more likely to be members of minority groups, those who choose not to vote are not much different in their attitudes toward the political process than those who do vote. According to the *NBC News/Wall Street Journal* poll, nonvoters are not an uninformed group. They know who the candidates are and something about their positions. As the presidential election campaign of 1992 heated up, the startling finding of the poll was that voters were thinking more like nonvoters; that is, that our political system is not working well.

In his book *The Decline of American Political Parties: 1952–1988,* Martin P. Wattenberg identifies the major functions of political parties in America as follows:[3]

1. "Generalizing symbols of identification and loyalty." The Republicans, sometimes called the Grand Old Party or GOP, have the elephant as their symbol. The symbol of the Democratic Party is the donkey. In decades of political cartooning few readers are not familiar with these symbols.

2. "Aggregating and articulating political interests." Each party builds a party platform (principles) upon which candidates run for office. In these platforms, parties seek to sharpen their differences with the opposing party while explaining why their positions are preferable. Platform statements also assuage diverse interest groups within the party.

3. "Mobilizing majorities in the electorate and in government." Political parties try to enlist the support of a majority of voters for their candidates. In government, political parties try to keep party members in Congress in line so that legislation they oppose is defeated and legislation they advocate is adopted. When the president and the majority of each house of Congress are of different parties, it may be difficult for either party to pursue its objectives. A stalemate may be the result.

4. "Socializing voters and maintaining a popular following." There are no standards of admission to a political party, no required dues, and even no obligation to vote for the party's candidate. Often one's family background, place of residence, level of education, occupation, and living style influence one's choice of a political party more than the details of the party's platform. Parties invite "grassroots" (people's) participation so that interested men and women may express their views and perhaps become political workers for their party.

5. "Organizing dissent and opposition." While the party in power may point with pride to its accomplishments, the party out of power persistently views with alarm the proposals of the party in power and warns of dire consequences if that party is not changed. In the conduct of public business, the party out of power serves as a watchdog over the party in power.

6. "Recruiting political leadership and seeking governmental offices." Since the major function of a political party is to win election, it needs to nourish men and women with political talent who may be put up for political office. The parties also screen candidates for thousands of important appointive offices that the party in power controls. In this way the politically faithful are rewarded for making victory possible.

7. "Institutionalizing, channeling, and socializing conflict." A spectrum of political viewpoints exists in each of the major political parties. The political parties must allow, even encourage, divergent views yet keep their members under the umbrella of the party. An example in the Republican party is the abortion issue—"right to life" Republicans urge a strong antiabortion stand while "right to choose" Republicans urge the party to back away from the issue.

8. "Overriding the dangers of sectionalism and promoting national interest." This function was difficult for the parties to perform in the nineteenth century when northern Democrats opposed slavery while southern Democrats sought to retain that "peculiar institution" (as Southerners described slavery). Different sectional and economic interests, for example, farmers and business people, may divide each party over questions of tariffs, farm subsidies, the regulation of labor and industry, and even foreign policy.

9. "Implementing policy objectives." Once in power, a political party must carry out the policies in its platform.

10. "Legitimizing decisions of government." Political parties must get its members to accept the legislation passed by Congress and signed by the president. If a segment of the party tries to challenge a measure, the major parties must gain a consensus for the decisions the government has reached.

11. "Fostering stability in government." The discipline a party imposes on its members in office encourages stability in government. Sometimes however one or more members break way from their party position on an issue and vote with the opposition. Moreover, political parties facilitate the transition from one administration to another.

In his farewell address, George Washington warned against "the baneful effects of the spirit of party" which, he went on to say, "serves always to distract the public councils and enfeeble the public administration. It agitates the community with ill-founded jealousies and false alarms; kindles the animosity of one part against another; foments occasional riot and insurrection. It opens the door to foreign influence and corruption."[4]

In these views, however, Washington proved to be shortsighted for at their best, American political parties make American government work. Political party leaders emerged despite President Washington's advice, and developed a concept of political parties that ". . . embraced the propositions that competition between two strong, unified, disciplined parties was not dangerous to a democracy but vital to its health and maintenance . . ."[5]

In spite of the enormous potential for democratic government, there is a public sense that American political parties are not as effective as they once were. The prominent political journalist David Broder wrote in the *Washington Post*, "The governmental system is not working because the political parties are not working."[6] What, if anything, is wrong with political parties today? What, if anything, should be done to reform them? Indeed, can they be reformed at all?

"In a world in which political scientists disagree on almost everything, there is remarkable agreement among the political science profession on the proposition that the strength of American political parties has declined significantly over the past several decades."[7] Gary Orren classifies the sources of political party decline: 1) changes among the American people; 2) the revolutionary impact of computers and television; and, 3) attempts to reform the parties. Let us examine the sources of party decline under each of these headings.

DEMOGRAPHIC CHANGES:
America has become a highly mobile society. When people do not stay in a community for a long time, they do not develop strong ties to their surroundings and cannot take advantage of the available political opportunities. The grassroots efforts of political parties falter as loyalty to a party is difficult to sustain.

As literacy increases, citizens grow less dependent on political party bosses who insist that they stay close to the adopted party line. Voters can read newspapers and journals of varied opinions and can, at times, argue convincingly for alternative positions. The growth in literacy is matched by the sophistication with which the party leadership tries to keep its members in line, but improved educational opportunities widen the horizons of voters, and reduce reliance on the party.

Early immigrants depended on parties for their jobs. Fear of losing their jobs was a powerful motivation for their voting allegiance to the party leadership. Moreover, when hard times came and people lost jobs or felt the pangs of hunger, the political party boss often handed out food baskets and other necessities. Political groups helped the immigrant get citizenship papers, establish residence, register to vote, secure a license to drive a car, open a shop, or peddle food or merchandise in the street.

However, with the growth of government assistance to the people, such party functions become less important. Unemployment compensation provides those out of work with modest funds while they search for new work. Food stamps aid those in poverty to shop at the supermarket for food. Medicaid extends medical help to some of the needy. Consequently, political parties no longer try to provide for the poor in exchange for their vote.

IMPACT OF TELECOMMUNICATIONS:
In an age without electronic media, candidates had to rely on personal appearances. These had to be few in number, especially in national campaigns. Mainly voters learned about the candidate from political party representatives who explained the program of the nominee.

Television changed all that. On the television screen the candidates present themselves directly to the people. The voters can see for whom they are being asked to vote. Does he or she look honest? Intelligent? How effective is he or she in public speaking, in explaining his or her views? How well might the candidate represent the nation in foreign affairs? The candidates' spouses are also drawn into the picture and voters can get a sense, perhaps, of the candidate as a person.

Once in office, a president can bypass the party and appeal directly to the people through television. The televised news conference, the speech on controversial issues given in prime time, the State of the Union Message, all are now prepared with an eye on the television camera even more than on the audience before the speaker. By reaching directly to the people, for all its potential for important communication between the president and the people, the effect is to further weaken party loyalty and discipline.

The only thing worse than being on television is *not* being on television. To be ignored by television is to be ignored by the electorate. Candidates go to great lengths to see that they are newsworthy enough to merit TV coverage. As never before, presidential candidates seek interviews on TV talk shows in order to get their message across. In the 1992 presidential campaign, Ross Perot announced that he was available as a potential candidate on a popular talk show. When the Democratic candidate, William Clinton, found himself being eclipsed by the meteoric rise of interest in Ross Perot, he went on late night television to demonstrate his competence playing the saxophone!

As the 1992 presidential campaign neared its end, all the candidates sought guest appearances on the morning talk shows and talk show hosts, for better or worse, replaced traditional journalists. Hosts lobbed "easy" questions to their guests while the viewers' call-in questions were often unsophisticated and easily parried. The TV picture truly became more important than a thousand words, and the "sound bite" more important than reasoned discussion. To be seen playing the saxophone was better than not being seen at all. The presidential candidates generated considerable interest among potential voters, but is it desirable for attempts at political enlightenment to become entertainment?

Computerized political polls assess the popularity of candidates at every turn. Polls help the candidate determine which issues are popular with the electorate, and how the last speech was received. Through sophisticated sampling of voters, the outcome of an election is known long before the election polls have closed. Since nothing succeeds like success, polls help sway the election in the direction of the more popular candidate.

IMPACT OF REFORM:

The cement that binds a political party together is the political job or patronage. This is the ability of a political leader to give government jobs at national, state, and local levels, to party faithful. However, when job seekers are incompetent, or required to kickback a portion of their salary to the political boss or to the treasury of the party, reform is inevitable.

In 1883, the Pendleton Act was passed by Congress and signed by Chester A. Arthur (1881–1885) who had become president after the assassination of President James A. Garfield. The law said that some jobs would be based on merit rather than party loyalty. An examination would be required to test the skills of job seekers. Over the years an increasing number of government jobs have been added to the classified or civil service ranks. All jobs are not classified, and there is still a substantial number to be awarded to party supporters, but the civil service has removed a large number of jobs from the control of political leaders. Once the party loses its means to reward devoted service, a further erosion of loyalty results.

When bribery of office holders was common, and voters were paid for voting the "right" way, and proxies (substitutes) cast the ballots of long deceased voters, political reform became necessary. The Australian or secret ballot was introduced to enable a voter to cast a ballot without fear of reprisal. At one time the political parties printed and distributed the ballots. Often the opposition slate of candidates did not even appear on the ballot! Little wonder that ticket splitting (voting for candidates of both parties) was the exception rather than the rule.

Today, voters pride themselves on how independent they are and ticket splitting has become the voters' great American game. Paradoxically the split ticket has the effect of pouring sand into the machinery of the Constitution and its mechanism of separation of powers, thus making the gears of government turn ever more slowly and, possibly, even grind to a halt.

To thwart the time-honored practice of choosing presidential candidates in the back rooms of the conventions, the direct primary became common practice. In a primary, candidates run for election among members registered in the party, and the victorious candidate in each state is awarded convention delegates in proportion to the number of votes the candidate won. As a result, while there continues to be a great deal of hoopla at the political conventions, witty political speeches, and martial music to rally the faithful, there are few faithful to be rallied. The nominee of the party has already been chosen by popular vote in the primary.

While such openness appears to be more democratic, it weakens the control of party leaders over the nominating process. The people, not the professionals, choose the party nominee. But is this desirable? James MacGregor Burns likens the primary to a football game in which the spectators (the amateurs), rather than the managers (the professionals), call the plays and select the players.[8] Under the convention system, political leaders could negotiate among themselves and choose the person they thought had the best chance to win or had the talents and experience needed. If political bosses in the Democratic Party had been more influential in 1992, it is unlikely that Bill Clinton would have been nominated for the presidency of the United States. His popularity in the Democratic Party primaries made his choice at the Democratic Convention inevitable. Choosing a candidate behind closed doors, in the legendary "smoke-filled" room, should not be romanticized;

nevertheless, parties were strengthened as professional politicians "cut a deal" based upon their judgment as to the candidate with the best chance of winning.

Party loyalty is further eroded by the practice of primary elections. Both the smoke-filled backroom and the direct primary have their shortcomings. But if party cohesion is necessary yet forces are eroding party loyalty, how will America be governed?

How to restore partisanship as a political virtue without destroying necessary political reforms is the dilemma of political life today. Adding to that dilemma is the problem of financing political campaigns. No political hopeful for any office can expect to attract the voters and get his or her message heard without a substantial "war chest." How shall funds be raised? Who shall contribute to it? How may such funds be spent? How can candidates and their parties be held accountable for political expenditures?

POLITICAL DOLLARS AND SENSE

For $1,500 you could have dined with President George Bush on April 27, 1992. You would have had pasta salad, beef tenderloin (donated by the American Meat Institute), asparagus, wild rice, and pastries, each from different regions of the country, all washed down with red and white wines from Washington State, mineral water contributed by Vichy Springs, and snifters of brandy donated by Jepson Vineyards, both of California. This is what 4,000 diners enjoyed at the President's Dinner, a gathering of important and wealthy Republican Party supporters. When all the money raised at this one dinner was counted, $8 million was added to the Republican war chest.[9]

Unlike political parties in many other countries, parties in the United States depend on voluntary contributions. "From torchlight parades to 'telethons,' someone has to pay expenses."[10] In 1952, $140 million was spent in the election campaigns of that year. These costs included electing a president and vice president, members of Congress, and candidates for state and local offices, as well as expenditures for and against ballot proposals of many kinds. By 1984, that sum had increased to $1 billion. By 1988, the costs in the campaign cycle of that year rose to $2 billion.[11] In the presidential campaign of 1992, the Democrats spent $71 million and the Republicans $62 million, while the independent candidate Ross Perot spent $59 million.[12]

Is this too much or not enough to spend on politics? In 1992, candidate Ross Perot bought his way into the campaign by spending a small fraction of his colossal wealth. Is there a danger for American democracy in such an example? While the sums spent on political campaigns are huge, they are but a small fraction of money spent on gambling or cosmetics. Nevertheless, the high cost of campaigns raises concern that the political process may be flawed. Has money become so influential, and the possibility of corruption so great that it threatens the integrity of the electoral process? And so, once again, the call to reform spending on political campaigns is heard. While the call is loud and clear, few reforms have proven more elusive than that of controlling campaign expenditures.

The single most important reason for increasing campaign costs is that as the size of the electorate grows, office seekers must reach a growing number of eligible voters. Campaign expenses mount as the right to vote is extended. Costs went up when universal white male suffrage became the norm. Voting rights won for women, blacks, and other minorities further broadened the electorate and increased the necessity for candidates to get their message understood by an ever widening circle of voters. But costs go up also because the most costly campaign is a losing one, and so candidates try to outspend one another in the hopes that the difference will mean victory.

What do candidates do with their money? In the beginning, printing costs were the greatest expense when political contests were conducted in the newspapers. Other forms of printing included advertisements and posters. Collectors of political memorabilia may have buttons, handkerchiefs, banners, songbooks, or log cabins (as in the 1840 campaign of William Henry Harrison), and split rails (as in the 1860 campaign of Abraham Lincoln). Transportation, from the horse and buggy to the railroad to the jet plane, is always a major cost especially since 1860 when presidential hopefuls first actively went out to meet the public.

After 1950, the major causes of the increased campaign expenditures were the costs of radio and television advertising, computer use, polling, and sophisticated fund-raising mailings. Prepared detailed reports on money raised and spent, as called for in The Federal Election Campaign Act of 1971 and amended in 1974, adds to political expenses. Because our parties are not ideological, that is, neither the Republican nor Democratic parties may be described as standing for a rather clearly identifiable political philosophy, many donors contribute to both parties as a way of hedging their bets and being on the winning side.

What do contributors hope to get for their money? Major donors look for jobs (as ambassadors, for example), influence, tax advantages, access to people in high office, or legislation designed to help them in their business. As one heavy contributor to the Republican party put it: "Unless you have money, you

72

can't move the locomotive. You have to get funds into the mechanism so you can work it."[13]

Because money may corrupt the political process, laws have been passed to try to regulate the amount of money spent, who may contribute, and the size of the contribution. However, because the political machinery cannot be run without the "grease" money supplies, the laws attempting to regulate political campaigns are notoriously complex and easily bypassed.

Widespread misuse of campaign funds was disclosed in the Watergate scandals. Consequently, a number of laws were passed in the 1970s in an attempt to reform the financing of political campaigns. As amended in 1974, the federal election law limits individuals to giving $1,000 per election to federal candidates. Corporations and trade unions may form Political Action Committees (PACs) to which employees or members may contribute $5,000. However, individuals may give $20,000 to the committees of national parties, but not to individual candidates. But in no case may any individual contribute more than $25,000 a year. The law also set limits on the amounts candidates and parties can spend in federal elections. In addition to requiring detailed reports, it set up a program of public funding of presidential campaigns.

The Federal Election Commission supervises campaigns for federal office. Its six members are appointed by the president and confirmed by the Senate. However, their task is not an easy one because the rules for campaign financing can be easily avoided. While direct giving to candidates is limited, funds can be contributed for purposes other than backing specific candidates. Money can be given to political parties to hire additional workers to prepare literature or TV commercials designed to get out the vote. An advertisement on television from the Democratic National Committee urging Democrats to vote in a presidential election is a legitimate expenditure beyond the limits on spending for the Democratic candidate. Dinners such as the April 1992 President's Dinner raises "soft money" which can be used for any number of activities to further the Republican effort to elect the president and Republican members of Congress.

In its 1976 decision in *Buckley v. Valeo*, the Supreme Court struck down as unconstitutional the limits on spending for congressional campaigns. The Court reasoned that "money talks" and so spending it to conduct a campaign for political office is covered by the First Amendment to the United States Constitution which protects freedom of speech. However, the Court upheld provisions of the 1974 amendments that restricted campaign giving. It argued that such limitation was justified as a means of protecting the electoral process from both "the actuality and appearance" of corruption. In this important decision, the Court ruled that if candidates for office voluntarily accepted public funds, then spending limits could likewise be imposed.

In order to broaden the base of political giving, Congress included in the Revenue Act of 1971 a provision that each taxpayer may channel $1 of his or her tax payment, or $2 if the tax is jointly filed, to a Presidential Election Campaign Fund. This is entirely voluntary and is not an additional payment, but rather a shifting of the taxpayers' dollars to finance an election rather than pay the Internal Revenue Service. The public funding of election campaigns is an idea that has been growing in momentum and may well be the next step in electoral reform. In 1992, the major party candidates each received about $50 million dollars in public money.

Since public funds are provided only for presidential campaigns, congressional office seekers may spend as much as they like. Political Action Committees (PACs), groups representing special interests such as accountants, doctors, automobile dealers, insurance agents, labor unions, and others, donated in 1992 $73.4 million to congressional candidates.[14] Because the bulk of the money went to those already in office (incumbents), there is general concern among those who would like to reform election financing, that new candidates with fresh ideas but limited funds may be unable to get a hearing before the electorate. Common Cause, a group concerned with political reform, has urged widespread changes in the way campaigns are financed. In particular this group seeks public funding of political campaigns.

Curbing campaign expenditures is an elusive goal because limitations may bar effective communication between the candidate and the voters. Do they really have this effect? Regulating expenditures may reduce the number of voters who turn out at the polls to vote. Does this threaten democracy? If political campaigns are subsidized by government, does this open the door to government controlled elections? These are some of the issues on campaign financing that remain unresolved. But how much more political party reform is needed? Are the shortcomings of American politics a failure of leadership or a failure of institutions, that is, of political parties?

During the course of America's political history, five major realignments of political parties have taken place. The first was in 1800 when Thomas Jefferson was elected president and the dominance of the Federalist party ended. In 1828, Andrew Jackson became president with the support of newly enfranchised male voters from the frontier states in the West and urban voters from factories of the East. The election

PARTY REALIGNMENT OR PARTY REFORM

of Abraham Lincoln to the presidency in 1860 led to the Civil War and with the Union victory, an indivisible nation was assured and slavery was terminated. In 1896, the election of William McKinley marked the victory of industrial capitalism over populist agriculture. The Great Depression, which began in 1929, led to the election of Franklin Roosevelt in 1932 and to the passage of welfare legislation and a more activist role for government in the affairs of people. Each of these critical elections in American history has led to a realignment of parties and to the emergence of new political leadership. The election of Bill Clinton to the presidency and the return of the Democrats to power and responsibility after a absence of twelve years could mark a similar political realignment. But what brings political party realignment about—political leadership or party reform? Can America be governed without parties? Let us see.

POLITICAL LEADERSHIP
Does the nation need new political leadership rather than reform? Does it need another Lincoln or Roosevelt to serve as a midwife for strengthened political parties? And, if there is such a political leader, how shall we recognize him or her? Both Lincoln and Roosevelt were essentially little-known, untried politicians at the time of their elections as president. But they did have the capacity to prod reluctant parties to serve the people's needs.

Perhaps such a leader is among us, one who can utilize the reforms of a party system to crystallize a political vision around which larger numbers of voters may wish to rally or debate. To rekindle the flame of political discourse is the mission of political leadership for our time. The advance of democracy requires political leadership of the highest order. While we wait for such leadership to emerge, what may be needed is the development of a structure, in or outside of political parties, to make political leadership possible.

PARTY REFORM

Tom Wicker, distinguished columnist of *The New York Times*, writes in an article entitled, "Let Some Smoke In," that widespread dissatisfaction with the presidential nominees in the campaign year of 1992 might have been avoided ". . . by permitting state parties once again to select delegates by any method they choose."[15]

While Tom Wicker is not urging that the reforms of the past twenty years be thrown out altogether, his view is that some combination of preferential presidential primary and some party deliberations would leave the national conventions open to identify candidates who may have a good chance of winning the presidency.

In addition to proposals to restore importance to the national party conventions which choose a presidential candidate and draft a party platform, proposals are also made to reform the entire process of choosing American presidents.

The hesitancy about reforming politics in America is not that Americans and their leaders believe that the system is perfect, but fear of the unintended consequences of reform. Those who have mastered the current political system are reluctant to change. Having climbed the political mountain, they do not wish to be pushed off the mountain top by reforms that may not serve them well. As a result, it may be that substantive reform to strengthen the two-party system is not possible without the parallel development of sophisticated political leadership. Can we then survive as a democratic society without political parties altogether?

77

POLITICS WITHOUT PARTIES

While politics without parties may appear to us to be impossible, we might remember that this was precisely the kind of circumstances the Founding Fathers of 1787 viewed as the ideal. Moreover, when political parties were strongest and held together by formidable political bosses such as Mayor James Curley of Boston or Mayor Richard Daley of Chicago, many voters cast their ballots as they were told. Is it not evidence of a sophisticated and knowledgeable electorate that voters now vote independently and choose their candidates based upon their own analysis? And, is it not a sign of voter sophistication if, instead of choosing to vote for all the candidates of one party, they split their vote by voting for the best person in any party? If political parties are no longer as strong as they once were, does this not encourage other men and women without strong political ties to run for political office? Will this open the nomination and election process to an ever wider array of talent?

Clearly these are desirable tendencies, yet if political parties wither away, the floodgates open up to dangers which threaten democracy itself. The erosion of the present political parties may encourage so many splinter groups to form that America may be too divided to govern. A colorful leader with wide appeal may come forward and urge that Americans trade democracy for stability. The breakdown of the party system encourages authoritarians and threatens democracy itself.

An informed electorate is to be preferred to an uninformed one. Pluralism and political and ethnic diversity are to be cherished. Yet how to do so without political fragmentation is today's urgent political business. Political parties need to be instruments of loyalty and reconciliation as well as vehicles for electing and reelecting their candidates. In a democracy a people get the kind of government they deserve. Weakened political parties did not develop all at once. Instead, over a period of nearly fifty years, the American people began to feel that their parties were becoming increasingly irrelevant to their lives. If in America there can be no democratic government without a party system, how then can we restore relevance to our political parties?

Many proposals have been made by political scientists, members of Congress, and by party leaders themselves. Among the more important suggestions for strengthening political parties are:

1. *Publicly finance political campaigns.*

2. *Reform or abolish the electoral college.*

3. *"Let some smoke in." That is, decrease reliance on the direct primary and reinvigorate party conventions at the local, state, and national levels by restoring authority to party leaders.*

4. *Facilitate and encourage straight party voting.*

5. *Strengthen the party out of power.*

Do they go far enough? Do we need to change the Constitution to make party government possible? If so, how far shall we go? Is amending the Constitution sufficient or is a new Constitution necessary? We will examine the last question in the final chapter of this book. However, in order for national discussion to take place on these and other issues, we must turn first to a discussion of the freedoms Americans enjoy under the Bill of Rights and related amendments.

FREE AT LAST: OR ARE WE?

In 1983, Matthew Fraser, an honor student and an especially fine speaker, delivered a speech nominating his friend for a high office in the student government at Bethel High in the state of Washington. He said: "I know a man who is firm—he is firm in his pants, he's firm in his shirt, his character is firm—but most of all his belief, in you, the students of Bethel, is firm. Jeff Kuhlman is a man who takes his point and pounds on it. If necessary, he'll take an issue and nail it to the wall."[1]

Because of sexual innuendoes in the speech Fraser was suspended from school, and he was no longer considered a speaker at his high school graduation. School authorities held that Fraser violated an important part of his high school's code of behavior which read: "Conduct which materially and substantially interferes with the educational process is prohibited, including the use of obscene, profane language or gestures."

The United States District Court in Washington forced the high school to allow Matthew to return to school, after serving two days of his suspension, and deliver the commencement address. The school administration appealed the ruling to the United States Court of Appeals, Ninth Circuit, which also decided in favor of Fraser. The school district appealed to the highest court in the land which in July 1986 (*Bethel School District, No. 403 v. Fraser*) handed down its decision.

If you were a member of the Supreme Court would you decide in favor of Fraser or against him?

The Supreme Court ruled against Fraser. Chief Justice Warren Burger, who wrote the decision for the Court, held that schools were instruments of the state and ". . . may determine that the essential lesson of civil, mature conduct cannot be conveyed in a school that tolerates lewd, indecent, or offensive speech such as that indulged in by this confused boy. The pervasive sexual innuendo in Fraser's speech was plainly offensive to both teachers and students—indeed, to any mature person." Chief Justice Burger continued, "The process of educating our youth for citizenship in public schools is not confined to books, the curriculum, and the civics class; schools must teach by example the shared values of a civilized social order."

But if the Chief Justice is right, how does his view square with the First Amendment which declares, "Congress shall make no law . . . abridging freedom of speech . . ."? Was the decision such as to have a chilling effect on students who want to exercise their rights to freedom of expression as well as other rights to which they are entitled? For a better understanding of the issues involved we will need to examine the Constitution of the United States more closely.

A LIVING CONSTITUTION

Ours is called a "living" Constitution because it is not the same document today that it was in 1789. The original wording has remained the same, but the words have been subject to interpretation and reinterpretation by the Supreme Court. Consequently, the meaning of the Constitution is substantially different today from what it was two hundred years ago. The United States Supreme Court has decided cases which have changed the Constitution. The following cases reveal the complexity involved in determining rights and the range of issues that come before the Court:

Brown v. the Board of Education of Topeka (1954). The Court ruled that separate schools for black and white children were inherently unequal and were a violation of Amendment XIV.

Roth v. the United States (1957). The Court held that obscene material was not protected by the First Amendment which guarantees freedom of speech. The Court defined obscene as "material utterly without redeeming social value."

Engel v. Vitale (1962). The Court ruled that public schools could not require children to recite a state composed prayer.

New York Times v. Sullivan (1964). The Court held that the First Amendment protected the press from libel suits (a court action brought against a publication for intentionally writing what is false) brought by public figures unless there was proof of malicious intent.

Miranda v. Arizona (1966). The court ruled that police must inform suspects before questioning that they have the right to remain silent, that anything they say may be used against them, and that they have a right to counsel.

United States v. New York Times (1971). The Court upheld the right of the *New York Times* and the *Washington Post* to publish the "Pentagon Papers" which detailed how the United States became involved in Vietnam.

Roe v. Wade (1973). The Court declared that a woman in the first trimester of pregnancy can decide to have an abortion, and state laws to the contrary are therefore unconstitutional.

Hazelwood School District v. Kuhlmeier (1988). The Supreme Court held that school authorities could not deny First Amendment rights to an editor of a school newspaper. Educators could not act as " 'thought police' stifling discussion of all but state-approved topics and advocacy of all but the official position."

R.A.V. v. St. Paul (1992). The Court ruled that "hate speech" (racial, sexual, or ethnic slurs) could not be silenced because of its content.

Lee v. Weisman (1992). The Court reaffirmed its ban on prayer in schools.

How far can freedom be safeguarded if we must rely on judicial interpretations of the Supreme Court to tell us what freedom is? The Supreme Court often reverses itself. Thus, when the *Miranda* decision was viewed as giving too much protection to the accused, the Court backed away but did not entirely repeal the *Miranda* ruling in a number of decisions. In decisions subsequent to *Roe v. Wade*, the Court has narrowed the opportunity to choose abortion but has not entirely repealed the decision.

Finley Peter Dunne (1867–1936), better known as "Mr. Dooley," a well-known cartoonist and observer of the Washington scene, made the caustic observation that "th' Supreme Court follows th' iliction (*sic*) returns." What he meant was that despite the efforts of the Court to remain above politics and the popular passions of the moment, the members of the Court could not help but be influenced by public opinion as expressed by voters.

Moreover, since the members of the Supreme Court are appointed for life, presidents can appoint to the Court members who represent their own political philosophies. These justices remain on the Court long after the presidents who appointed them

83

have left office. As a result, sometimes the Court fails to reflect changing conditions and may appear insensitive to the needs of society. During the early years of the New Deal (1933–1937) under Franklin D. Roosevelt, the "nine old men," as they were jeeringly called, declared unconstitutional many of the reforms the president and Congress adopted to meet the needs of a depression-racked society. Not until a number of members of the Court retired was the constitutionality of New Deal measures sustained. In view of the pressures to which the Court is subject, how effectively does it protect the liberties of Americans?

THE LIBERTIES OF AMERICANS

Although the Declaration of Independence declared that people had "unalienable" rights to life, liberty, and the pursuit of happiness, it did not guarantee such rights. They are, however, embodied in the first ten amendments to the Constitution, collectively called the Bill of Rights. A metaphor for the role of the Bill of Rights is a traffic light which tells government how far it may go and when it must stop coercing the nation's people.

While traffic lights may operate automatically, the prerogatives of government are not automatic. For one thing, it is not possible to list the liberties of Americans for all time. For another, personal liberties are not absolute, but are always in conflict with the liberties of others. Your right to swing your arm is limited by how close it gets to another person's nose! In the United States, citizens rely on the United States Supreme Court to balance the needs of government with the needs of freedom.

The Constitution was first drafted without provision for a bill of rights. Since many state constitutions contained a bill of rights, there was grave concern that no such provision was made by the framers of the Constitution in their original draft. Why not?

Writing in *The Federalist* No. 84, Alexander Hamilton sought to explain why no bill of rights was necessary. He insisted that the Constitution itself adequately protected the liberties of Americans. Among the more important examples he pointed out were the following:

1. *Congress may not suspend the writ of* habeas corpus *which prevents the indefinite imprisonment of a person without a speedy investigation.*

2. *Congress may not pass a bill of attainder or* ex post facto *law. The first is a law that convicts (attaints) a person of a crime without benefit of a trial. The second is one that inflicts penalties (jail, fines, executions) for deeds which were not illegal at the time they were performed.*

3. *Trial shall be by jury.*

4. *Treason shall be limited to actually making war against the United States or giving aid and comfort to the nation's enemies.*

5. *No religious test may be required for any office.*

6. *No title of nobility shall be granted by the United States.*

Hamilton went on to ".... affirm that bills of rights ... are not only unnecessary in the proposed Constitution but would even be dangerous. .... Why declare that things shall not be done which there is no power to do? Why, for example, should it be said that the liberty of the press shall not be restrained, when no power is given by which restrictions may be imposed?"[2] While Hamilton's views have some merit, and most of the drafters of the Constitution agreed with them, Thomas Jefferson urged that a bill of rights be added to the Constitution and popular sentiment in favor was so great that the Constitution probably could not have been ratified without one.

Today, it is not the necessity of a bill of rights that is debated but the adequacy of those rights and liberties in view of circumstances that the framers of the Constitution could not contemplate. Moreover, is the Bill of Rights, adopted in the eighteenth century (passed by Congress on September 25, 1789, and ratified by three-fourths of the states on December 15, 1791), adequate to serve the needs of the Americans in the twenty-first century?

The text of the Bill of Rights may be found in the Appendix to this volume. Here they are briefly summarized:

Amendment I forbids Congress from enacting laws establishing religion or prohibiting the free exercise of religious worship. In the words of Jefferson this portion of the amendment separates church and state. Freedom of speech, press, assembly, and petition may not be abridged.

Amendment II guarantees the right of Americans to bear arms.

Amendment III prohibits the quartering of soldiers in private homes in peacetime without the owner's consent.

Amendment IV prohibits unreasonable searches and seizures.

Amendment V forbids the deprivation of life, liberty, or property without due process of law. It goes on to forbid being tried twice for the same offense (double jeopardy) and forbids government form forcing an individual to testify against oneself.

Amendment VI guarantees a speedy and impartial trial and a local jury in criminal cases.

Amendment VII provides for a jury trial in civil actions.

Amendment VIII prohibits excessive bail, fines, and cruel and unusual punishments.

Amendment IX declares that rights not specifically listed should not be considered denied.

Amendment X affirms that powers not expressly delegated to the federal government are reserved to the states and the people.

The rights enumerated here marked a great advance for the world of the eighteenth century. There were, however, important aspects of the human condition which should have concerned the authors of the first ten amendments to the Constitution but which were unresolved by them. The Bill of Rights failed to deal with the evils of slavery. The plight of men and women who worked without pay on farms and plantations, in shops and factories, and as household servants and nursemaids was neglected. The slaves were considered to be property rather than people. As property, they were bought, sold, and mortgaged. On these appalling abuses the Bill of Rights was silent.

Nor were women mentioned in the Bill of Rights. Since the determination of eligibility to vote was left to the states, the states denied voting rights to women for many years. Moreover, because states determined who would have suffrage (the right to vote), states could and did impose property tests for voting. In this way, the poor were denied the right to vote. We must not be too harsh on James Madison, who is known as the Father of the Bill of Rights, for his skill in getting them drafted and adopted. Those who were initially denied protection of the Bill of Rights could and did in later years draw on its provisions to redress their grievances.

In order to make up for some of the shortcomings in the Bill of Rights, other amendments were, from time to time, adopted which have served to strengthen the rights of Americans. These include the following:

Amendment XIII (1865) ends slavery and involuntary servitude.

Amendment XIV (1868) provides due process and equal protection under the laws and prohibits the abridgment of privileges and immunities of citizens by the states.

Amendment XV (1870) says the right to vote may not be denied on account of race, color or previous condition of servitude.

Amendment XVII (1913) provides for the direct election of United States Senators by popular vote of the people.

Amendment XIX (1920) gives the right to vote to women.

Amendment XXIV (1964) abolishes a poll tax. (This is a tax on the right to vote imposed by some states.)

Amendment XXVI (1971) gives the right to vote to eighteen-year-olds.

Despite these additional amendments, are the standards for human rights as outlined in a document written in the eighteenth century adequate for the twenty-first century?

THE BILL OF RIGHTS AND AN ORWELLIAN WORLD

Comb your hair, put on some decent clothes, and a smile on your face. The videophone is at hand. Getting ready for a telephone call on the videophone may be as time consuming as getting ready for a date. To be able to see via videophone whom we are calling is as revolutionary an advance in telecommunications as radio, television, and the computer.

Is the videophone a potential benefactor of limitless possibilities, or will it become as intrusive as commercials on TV? What safeguards does one have against obscene videopictures? Is separation of church and state violated if religious groups use videophones to solicit converts? If the videophone is used for instructional purposes, are providers of such instruction entitled to public funds destined for education? The Supreme Court of the United States will assuredly be called upon to decide these and other questions relating to emerging technology. But in their decisions they will have to rely upon the United States Constitution.

In his book *1984* the English author George Orwell may have been a decade or more ahead of his time when he visualized a world in which emerging technologies threaten liberty. A number of examples will serve to illustrate how ambiguous traditional concepts of freedom have become.

So far have telecommunications advanced that the dividing line between the written and the verbal becomes obscure. A case in point is electronic mail. You sit before your modem-equipped computer and dash off a memo informing your friend that you will be a half hour late for an appointment. E-Mail, as it is called, can be wiped off the screen and made to disappear almost as quickly as your voice disappears when you put down the phone. What if your friend shows up at the appointed time and accuses you of not being on time? What proof do you have that you did send a note indicating a time change? What if you are a person of some prominence and proof of where you were becomes a matter of grave importance?

The Federal Records Act requires the government to preserve important documents for later generations to study. But is E-Mail a written document and so subject to the law, or is it merely replacing the telephone call which is not subject to the Federal Records Act? Because E-Mail is becoming more widely used at all levels of government, it is critical to future generations to determine if electronic mail is a document that governments must preserve. Librarians and historians worry that if E-Mail circulating among important personages in and out of government may vanish without a trace, then a whole era may be lost to future analysis.

Other challenges to liberty because of technological advances include the following:

- *People's actions can now be photographed at so great a distance that surveillance can not possibly be detected. Is this an invasion of privacy and does the Constitution offer us protection?*
- *Microphones can be concealed in tiepins so that one may be totally unaware that one's conversation is being recorded. Does the Constitution permit or prohibit such eavesdropping?*
- *The letter you write can be read without the envelope being opened. What does the United States Constitution have to say?*
- *Employers interested in the leisure activities of employees may use electronic devices to monitor their behavior. Do such employees have any constitutional redress if they find out they are being watched?*
- *Your poor showing on SATs (scholastic achievement tests) may haunt you forever since records of your performance are maintained for so long a time that someone interested in your score could possibly find it. Is this an example of "unreasonable search and seizure" (search of your files and seizure of your records) against which we are protected by the Fourth Amendment to the United States Constitution?*
- *If AIDS (Acquired Immune Deficiency Syndrome) is spread primarily through promiscuous sexual behavior and intravenous drug use, may the government, through the use of electronic surveillance, monitor the sexual behavior and drug use of its people in an attempt to control the spread of the disease? Is such a step constitutional?*

- *The advance of medical technology has made the very meaning of birth, life, and death less clear. When, if at all, can an organ be taken from a fetus? Is a fetus a person within the meaning of the law? Is abortion the right of a mother to choose, or is it murder as some contend? Can a person who is suffering with a terminal illness be assisted to die? To whom does the infant of a surrogate mother belong? What is the legal status of test-tube babies? Can a person found guilty of chronic violence be forced to take a drug that would make him or her more law-abiding?*

As the Bill of Rights becomes increasingly remote from the historical context in which it was written, opportunity exists for the unbridled expansion of influence of the Supreme Court which interprets the Constitution. Is this a good thing? Can the Court become arbitrary and dictatorial? The Founding Fathers could not even guess at recent scientific and technological developments. Even thinking about writing a new constitution is for the purpose of assuring that the rights of Americans in the emerging century will be assured.

Technology changes rapidly and the law changes slowly. The Constitution's freedoms of speech and press were adequate for a time when print was the only medium of expression. They may not be adequate for a period of revolution in telecommunications. Freedom of speech and press in their conventional forms has essentially been won. However, the fight for equal freedom of communication in radio, film, television, and computers has only just begun. Because the dominant resource of the next century may be information, freeing information technology in all its forms is the struggle yet to be won. "The onus is on us to determine whether free societies in the twenty-first century will conduct electronic communication under the conditions of freedom established for the domain of print through centuries of struggle, or whether that great achievement will become lost in a confusion about new technologies."[3]

America has long been viewed as a land of opportunity. We have prided ourselves on the fact that through the Bill of Rights and other provisions of the Constitution, we have tried to level the "playing field" for all people. But have we in fact done so? Of what value is freedom of speech to people who are hungry? Of what value is freedom to worship as one wishes if one has no shelter? The Bill of Rights, a product of the generation in which it was written, was concerned with civil and political rights. It was a negative document in that it essentially told the people what the government may not do. It did not say anything about what the government ought to do, or indeed, whether it ought to do anything at all.

Because it was not possible to list all the rights to which Americans were entitled, the writers of the Bill of Rights incorporated a rather open-ended amendment which implies that from time to time, other rights may be incorporated. Amendment IX declares: "The enumeration in the Constitution of certain rights shall not be construed to deny or disparage others retained by the people." What other rights did Mr. Madison and his colleagues have in mind? We may never know, but if the first generation of rights were concerned with political and civil safeguards, might the second generation of rights be appropriately concerned with social and economic safeguards? Let us see.

NURTURING
RIGHTS

On January 11, 1944, with victory in Europe and the Pacific assured, President Franklin D. Roosevelt proposed a new Bill of Rights for the nation. "This Republic," he declared, "had its beginning, and grew to its present strength, under the protection of certain inalienable political rights—among them the right of free speech, free press, free worship, trial by jury, freedom from unreasonable searches and seizures. They were our rights to life and liberty."

However, he went on, *"As our Nation has grown in size and stature . . . as our industrial economy expanded—these political rights proved inadequate to assure us equality in the pursuit of happiness.*

"We have come to a clear realization of the fact that true individual freedom can't exist without economic security and independence. 'Necessitous men are not free men.' People who are hungry—people who are out of a job—are the stuff of which dictatorships are made.

"In our day these economic truths have become accepted as self-evident. We have accepted, so to speak, a second Bill of Rights under which a new basis of security and prosperity can be established for all—regardless of station, race, or creed.

"Among these are:

"The right to a useful and remunerative job in the industries or shops or mines of the Nation;

"The right to earn enough to provide food and clothing and recreation;

"The right of farmers to raise and sell their products at a return which will give them and their family a decent living;

"The right of every businessman, large and small, to trade in an atmosphere of freedom from unfair competition and domination by monopolies at home or abroad;

"The right of every family to a decent home;

"The right to adequate medical care and the opportunity to achieve and enjoy good health;

"The right to adequate protection from the eco-

nomic fears of old age and sickness and accident and unemployment;
"And finally, the right to a good education."[4]

If the first generation of rights has to do with political and civil liberties, the second generation of rights has to do with those that nurture people so that they may avail themselves of all other rights and develop their human potential. The American Constitution is concerned with onslaughts against the individual by those who would limit expression, or erode the safeguards of fair and speedy jury trials, or interfere with the right of people not to incriminate themselves. Nurturing rights protect individuals from personal, economic, and social disasters.

But President Roosevelt was wrong. He described his economic and social rights for America as "self-evident." They are not. Laws governing social security, unemployment insurance, and medical benefits try to nurture men and women, but as the twentieth century draws to a close, nurturing rights have not yet found their way into the Constitution of the United States. But should they? Are they the natural rights of which Jefferson wrote when he drafted the Declaration of Independence? Are these rights at all or merely minimal goals? Are they achievable? Are such rights the responsibility of state and/or local governments? Since they are not cost-free, who pays?

"Life, liberty, and the pursuit of happiness," is a goal each individual is free to pursue. But what if, in such individual pursuits, some are left behind? The Founding Fathers believed that individual effort, on a vast continent with limitless resources, could satisfy at least minimal needs. But, if minimal needs are not met, where does responsibility lie? The debate about such goals presented to Congress almost fifty years ago, continues to rage.

American ideals of individual liberty have swept

94

the world. "People everywhere want to share the American experience, to get a bite at the apple of individualism," Ben Wattenberg, a senior fellow at the American Enterprise Institute told a conference.[5] Yet, even as they have adopted important elements of the Bill of Rights, many countries have moved beyond it to include nurturing rights as well. As telecommunications and the jet plane draw the world's countries ever closer, liberty for the people in one country is threatened if liberty for people in other countries is denied.

During and immediately after World War II, the United States led in making the idea of rights universal. President Franklin Roosevelt in his speech to Congress (1941) identified "Four Freedoms" he believed were "attainable in our time and generation . . . everywhere in the world." "The first," he declared, "is freedom of speech and expression. . . . The second is freedom of every person to worship God in his own way. . . . The third is freedom from want. . . . The fourth is freedom from fear. . . ." Eleanor Roosevelt, wife of the president, was the leader in drafting the Universal Declaration of Human Rights.

International statements on human rights incorporate many, but by no means all, of the protections afforded by the United States Constitution and the Bill of Rights. However, international statements often make explicit what in the American documents is implicit. Thus, the right to change one's residence, to travel, to leave the country and return to it, the right to marry a person of one's choice, to establish a family, the right of parents to guide the moral education of children are among the rights incorporated in the Universal Declaration of Human Rights, the International Covenant on Civil and Political Rights, and the International Covenant on Economic, Social and Cultural Rights. International rights' declarations also prohibit torture, and accord women and children special rights.

While many international statements of human rights may appear to go father than do parallel expressions in the United States, they do not in fact do so. The United States Constitution cannot be suspended. Many international charters permit the suspension of constitutions during periods of emergency. More than one authoritarian government has suspended the nation's constitution. Moreover, many international charters that incorporate nurturing rights do so with the view that government can intercede to make these economic and social rights a reality. The United States proceeds from a different perspective. Jefferson said that government is best which governs least, and Americans approach rights from the point of view of minimalist government intervention. The hand that guarantees a job may also be the hand that takes it away. The government that allows its citizens to travel, also has the implicit power to take that right away.

The American influence on international human rights has been inconsistent. "Our trumpet in the cause of human rights has . . . been muffled by our continued failure to ratify principal international human rights covenants and conventions. But if our political influence has been uneven, the significance of our example . . . is beyond dispute."[6] The eyes of the world remain on the American example—on rights achieved and, more importantly, on the endless struggle to preserve them, and to reinterpret them in the light of changing standards, global responsibilities, and technological developments.

In Jefferson's view, the framers of the Constitution did not believe their work was "too sacred to be touched." Possibly, they would be surprised to find that the Constitution they wrote over two hundred years ago was still the supreme law of a land vastly different from the one they knew. If they were to draft a constitution for today's America, what would they change? How would they go about it?

They might reconsider the provision they made for amending the Constitution, and question whether the provision was still adequate. With the precedent of 1787 to guide them, they might even suggest a second constitutional convention and propose a new constitution altogether. Would such a convention be timely? Would such a convention be desirable? In the chapter that follows we will examine some of these questions.

DO WE NEED A NEW CONSTITUTION?

"Do you care which party wins?" an interviewer asked a number of representative Americans. Here are some of the answers they gave:

- *A worker in a Pittsburgh mattress factory: "Doesn't make any difference to me. I am not interested in stuff like that. I don't listen to nothing; I don't even read about politics in the paper."*
- *A fisherman from Minnesota: "Not a bit . . . don't believe in politics."*
- *Wife of a laborer in Georgia: "I guess you'd call me not caring since I've never voted . . ."*[1]

Making matters worse is the paradox, while Americans love democracy, they hate politics and politicians. Mark Twain (1835–1910) set the tone when he noted, "There is no native criminal class in America, other than politicians."[2]

Clearly something is amiss if so many Americans are apathetic about politics. Is it that government makes no difference? Or is it that the Constitution, written more than 200 years ago, no longer speaks to

Americans as it once did? If so, can the Constitution be changed? Is a new Constitution needed?

The framers of the Constitution, who were perhaps reluctant to see their beloved creation changed without careful deliberation, made the amending process difficult. According to Article V of the United States Constitution, amendments must be proposed and ratified (approved). An amendment may be proposed in one of two ways:

1. *By a two-thirds vote of each house of Congress.*

2. *By a national convention called by Congress at the request of two-thirds of the state legislatures.*

An amendment must also be ratified in one of two ways:

3. *By the legislatures of three-fourths of the states.*

4. *By conventions held in three-fourths of the states.*

Most amendments have been proposed by a two-thirds vote of each house of Congress and ratified by the legislatures of three-fourths of the states. Since 1921, Congress has set a time limit of seven years during which states may ratify. The president's signature is not required and the president may not veto an amendment that has been lawfully proposed and ratified. The Supreme Court may not declare an amendment unconstitutional.

Since 1789, there have been over 5,000 proposed amendments to the United States Constitution, but only twenty-six have been adopted. Does this mean that the Constitution has changed very little in over 200 years? Although the wording of the Constitution has changed very little, the way we are governed has changed a great deal. If the framers of the Constitution could convene in Philadelphia today, they would see a very different political process.

Article VI, Section 2 of the Constitution declares: "This Constitution, and the laws of the United States which shall be made in pursuance thereof . . . shall be the supreme law of the land. . . ." It is not the Constitution standing alone that is the supreme law; it is also laws that are passed by Congress and signed by the president as well. When Congress passes a law it, in effect, changes the way we are governed. The new law may be challenged by those who think that it violates the Constitution. Most laws go unchallenged. Laws that are challenged and are declared by the Supreme Court to be constitutional become the supreme law of the land. Laws that are declared to be unconstitutional are invalidated. A new law that takes into account the concerns of the Supreme Court may be passed by Congress and signed by the president or an amendment may be adopted that changes the wording of the Constitution itself.

Legislation governing wages and hours, social security, unemployment compensation, and provision for health care were all adopted by Congress and signed by the president and became the laws of the land. For better or worse, America became a welfare state within the framework of the Constitution without formal amendment. The framers of the Constitution never envisioned this revolutionary concept of government.

Significant departures in government, such as those that occurred during the New Deal era of Franklin D. Roosevelt (1933–1945), require a strong president with a popular mandate. But such executive popularity and strong leadership do not often exist. Indeed, they are the exception rather than the rule. Too often, proposed reforms are deferred when there appears to be little consensus among the people for radical change. Some presidents are unwilling to rock "the ship of state" or risk their chances for reelection.

Other presidents may be unsure of the direction in which to go.

Modern technology draws countries ever closer, and the nation is affected by tumultuous events from afar. Many people think that structural reforms of such magnitude are needed that the unthinkable must be considered; namely, writing a new constitution for an America whose world is vastly different from that the framers of the original Constitution.

America was the first nation to draft a written constitution. It is the oldest framework of government still functioning in the world. Although another constitutional convention has never been convened to revise the United States Constitution, more than 230 state constitutional conventions have been held. Six states have adopted a half a dozen or more complete revisions of their constitutions. The state of Louisiana has adopted a total of eleven new constitutions.[3]

Since the end of the Reconstruction (1876), about forty serious proposals have been made for a major constitutional revision.[4] Few have been taken seriously. None have aroused the imagination or the interest of the people. A few proposals have included complete or substantial drafts for a new constitution.

In 1942, as the title of his book indicates, Henry Hazlitt asked, "A New Constitution Now?"[5] Hazlitt answered affirmatively and made a number of startling proposals. For one thing, Congress would be empowered to choose the president. The president would have the power to dissolve the Congress. The vice presidency would be abolished. Representatives would have a staggered four-year term with one-quarter of the House elected each year. State governors and legislators, not the president, would choose members of the Supreme Court. The president would have the power to veto individual items in the budget. In place of the amending process, the president would institute a referendum among the people for proposed changes.

In 1945, Thomas Finletter, a Democrat, a former United States ambassador to the North Atlantic Treaty Organization, and secretary of the air force, proposed that the president be empowered to dissolve Congress and call for new elections for members of Congress as well as the president. The president and members of Congress would serve concurrent six year terms. To minimize or even avoid clashes between the legislative and executive branches, he proposed a joint executive-legislative cabinet which he felt could be adopted by joint resolution of the House and Senate. Finletter was impressed with how the world had changed as a result of World War II and wondered if the Constitution was adequate to meet the needs of the postwar world. "Can the means of government remain the same," he wondered, "when its ends have so greatly increased in scope?"[6]

Leland Baldwin, a distinguished historian, proposed a unicameral (one house) legislature which the president could dissolve and call for a new election. Two hundred members of Congress would be elected for five years. Moreover, the president could appoint enough at-large members of Congress so that the president's party would always have a 55 percent majority in Congress. Baldwin would also abolish the vice presidency, the electoral college, and the United States Senate. He would reconstitute the Senate as ". . . a court of last resort . . . charged with guardianship of the public welfare and a limited oversight of legislation."[7] He proposed that the presiding officer of the reconstituted Senate be the chief justice of the Supreme Court.

In Baldwin's view ". . . the States are no longer

viable," he declared, "they are antiquated, clumsy, antipathetic toward each other, and no longer capable of performing their functions."[8] He believed that the powers of states should be reduced even as some states be enlarged and others consolidated into more viable units.

In 1974, Charles M. Hardin, a distinguished political scientist, proposed that senators, representatives, and the president all serve concurrent four-year terms. He argued that 150 members, elected at-large and divided between the parties in such a way that the president's party would always have a clear majority, be added to the size of the House of Representatives. Presidential candidates should be nominated by party committees made up of members of the House. To limit the president's veto power, a majority of the House alone could override the presidential veto. The Senate would be radically weakened and deprived of its power to approve treaties. Something of a "loyal opposition" would be established in which the leader of the party out of power would have membership on congressional committees, an official residence, and funds for staff and travel.[9]

Also in 1974, Rexford G. Tugwell, who had been a liberal New Dealer and a member of Franklin Roosevelt's informal body of advisors known as the "Brain Trust," proposed a far-reaching constitutional revision. Tugwell devoted over ten years to a study of the Constitution and drafted specific language for one.[10] He was convinced that a complete rewriting of the Constitution was necessary to make government more responsive to changing conditions. His proposed constitution included an expansion of rights and liberties, a form of parliamentary government, an office for economic and political planning, revising federal and state relationships, and provision for a group of administrators to help the government become more efficient. Along with others who framed full-scale proposals, he incorporated aspects of the "unwritten constitution" such as organization of Congress, role of political parties, and the place of America in the global community.

Proposing new constitutions is an exercise in courage if not futility because it is unlikely to gather widespread support among either the people or the politicians. However, such broad thinking helps us to develop a consensus around corrections in midcourse without scrapping our Constitution or embarking on an uncharted political sea. But what changes do Americans want? Let us see.

The voice of the people is "an echo chamber," declared the distinguished political scientist V. O. Key. "If the people can choose only from among rascals, they are certain to choose rascals."[11] "Fed a steady diet of buncombe (nonsense)," he continued, "the people may come to expect and to respond with highest predictability to buncombe."[12] What he meant was that what the people urge is but an echo of what they hear or read in the media. And, since that message is mixed, it is not surprising that the voice of the people on constitutional change is also mixed as the following data indicate:

The people tend to hold the Constitution in such awe that in response to surveys they insist that "it should not be tampered with."[13] Yet in response to the question: "Are there any amendments you would like to see made to the Constitution?" of a CBS/New York Times poll May 11–14, 1987 (the last time the question was asked), 75 percent favored an equal rights amendment, 85 percent favored a balanced budget amendment, while 69 percent favored an amendment that would permit organized prayer to be said in public schools.[14]

If the public is ambivalent about changing the Constitution, some scholars, journalists, and students of government believe that some important changes need to be made. Among the more important are proposals to strengthen political parties, reform election procedures, modify separation of powers, and improve government efficiency.

TO STRENGTHEN POLITICAL PARTIES:

1. *Strengthen political parties by providing for public financing of national parties and political campaigns; limit the amount of money congressional candidates may spend on election campaigns.*

2. *De-emphasize the primaries and give the parties a greater role in selecting nominees for office.*

TO REFORM ELECTION PROCEDURES:

3. *End split-ticket voting by requiring that voters choose a slate of candidates from the president and vice president through House and Senate nominees.*

4. *Abolish the electoral college and institute direct popular election of the president.*

5. *Replace current state primaries with regional ones to reduce the number of primaries.*

6. *Abolish the vice presidency.*

TO MODIFY SEPARATION OF POWERS:

7. *Permit chairpersons of congressional committees to head cabinet departments in order to end the stalemate in government brought about by excessive checks and balances. A variation is to require the president to choose cabinet officers from the congressional leadership.*

8. *Permit presidents to dissolve Congress and call for new elections as prime ministers do in governments with a parliamentary system (e.g. Britain or Israel.)*

9. *Permit Congress to remove presidents who have lost the power to govern.*

10. *Limit the president to a single six-year term of office. On the other hand, some propose repealing Amendment XXII which limits the president to two terms.*

11. *Limit the terms of Senators and Representatives to twelve years.*

TO IMPROVE EFFICIENCY IN GOVERNMENT:

12. *Allow the president to veto individual items in the federal budget, a power that most state governors now have. The federal government, like many state governments, should be required to balance its budget.*

13. *Redraw state boundaries.*

14. *Permit treaties to be approved by less than a two-thirds majority of the Senate.*

15. *Establish a highly competent corps of civil servants to administer major agencies of government and keep them independent of political partisanship.*

16. *Make amending the Constitution easier.*

These are but some of the changes that have been proposed in the Constitution of the United States. To effect these or other changes or to draft a new constitution, some people urge that a new constitutional convention be convened.

SHOULD A CONSTITUTIONAL CONVENTION BE CALLED

On September 15, 1787, the last day of the Constitutional Convention, George Mason of Virginia noted that only Congress had the power to propose constitutional amendments. He considered this unfair and that the people, through their state legislatures, ought to have an alternate way of proposing amendments. And so, his proposal to require Congress to convene a constitutional convention at the request of the legislatures of two-thirds of the states was adopted.

This method of amending the Constitution has never been used because what unintended consequences might flow from a constitutional convention are unknown. Will a constitutional convention limit its work to the purpose for which it was convened, or will it follow the example of those who in 1787 met to *amend* the Articles of Confederation but, quite illegally, remained to write a new Constitution for the United States of America?

The American people face a formidable dilemma. Should a constitutional convention be called to make things better at the risk of unleashing uncontrollable forces that could make things worse? Or, should a constitutional convention be avoided until there is a political crisis which threatens the very life of the nation? Senator Robert Kennedy called this provision for changing the Constitution ". . . a darker side to the amendment process. . . ."[15] Yet, the prominent author, Gore Vidal, referred to the same provision as "The founders' last gift to us . . . the machinery to set things right."[16] Who is right?

An amendment to require a balanced budget has been proposed by the states but has thus far fallen just short of the required two-thirds needed for the convening of a constitutional convention. Were this to happen, it would be the only constitutional convention ever called since 1787. Irrespective of the merits or shortcomings of a balanced budget amendment, should such a convention be called?

Richard Rovere suggested in *The New Yorker* that the convention method of amending the Constitution might reinstate slavery or segregation, throw out the Bill of Rights, eliminate the due process clause in Amendment XIV or even do away with the Supreme Court itself.[17] Richard Rovere may have been writing with tongue in cheek because these risks are remote.

THE RISKS OF A CONSTITUTIONAL CONVENTION

Nevertheless, the very idea of a new constitutional convention strikes fear in the hearts of many.

The constitutional question is whether or not Congress can insist that the proposed constitutional convention deal with a single issue. Some noted scholars believe that it can. Others of equal prominence believe that once a constitutional convention is called, Congress will be powerless, despite legislation to the contrary, to limit deliberations to a single issue. Since such a convention, in effect, stands above the Congress, the courts, or the presidency, there will be nothing to prevent such an assembly from proposing an amendment prohibiting abortion, requiring prayer in school, a balanced budget, or school busing. The convention can even rewrite the Constitution of the United States.

Calling a constitutional convention may cause revolutionary complications. The following scenario, though remote, is possible. The necessary two-thirds vote of the state legislature is obtained and Congress, as required, calls a constitutional convention. The convention refused to heed congressional insistence that it confine its deliberations to a single issue. Instead, it drafts a new constitution and submits it to three-fourths of the state legislatures or state conventions, who in turn adopt the proposed constitution. Under circumstances such as these how is such a confrontation resolved? Violence, not unlike that which is common to the most unstable governments, may result if the sitting Congress which authorized the convention in the first place refuses to give up its power.

While such an event is unlikely, it is possible. In 1787, the nation believed that writing a new constitution was necessary during that period of time historians call the "Critical Period." In our own day, are we in such critical straits that convening a new constitutional convention is worth the risk? Are our institutions of government—Congress, the presidency, the Supreme Court, separation of powers, the federal system—so removed and unresponsive to the people that changing them would be welcome? Are our freedoms so threatened that a new Bill of Rights would be appropriate? And, there is no assurance that a constitutional convention would indeed expand our rights and liberties: it could reduce them. While the First Amendment guarantees freedom of speech and press, the free exercise of religion, and petition and assembly, the wording of a new constitution may not be so sweeping.

Other questions relating to constitutional convention are: How will the delegates be chosen? Who will pay them? How long should the convention last? Will the vote be by individual delegate or by state? How many votes will it require to adopt an amendment—A simple majority? A two-thirds or a three-fourths vote?

Catherine Drinker Bowen's book about the proceedings of the Constitutional Convention of 1787 is entitled *Miracle at Philadelphia*.[18] What if no miracle occurs? Who are the men and women today to match Washington, Madison, Hamilton and others of that assembly of notables who framed the Constitution? But if there are risks, there are also opportunities; namely, to draft a constitution which may be more responsive to the needs of the twenty-first century.

Thomas Jefferson explained, in 1816, " . . . each generation . . . has the right to choose for itself the form of government it believes most promotive of its own happiness . . . it is for the peace and good of mankind that a solemn opportunity of doing this every nineteen or twenty years should be provided by the constitution." The approach of the twenty-first century may provide "a solemn opportunity" for the na-

THE OPPORTUNITIES OF A CONSTITUTIONAL CONVENTION

tion to follow Jefferson's advice and convene a constitutional convention.

Since the Constitution was written there have been more than 400 calls for a constitutional convention, from every one of the fifty states. Ninety percent of these calls were made in the twentieth century and 50 percent were made since the 1960s.[19] While none of them have mustered enough support to require Congress to convene a convention, nevertheless, the existence of a method of bypassing Congress to amend the Constitution serves as a prod on members of Congress to propose changes.

Calls for a national convention preceded Amendment XVII requiring the direct election of Senators, Amendment XXI repealing prohibition, Amendment XXII limiting the president to two terms, and Amendment XXV outlining the succession to the presidency. When the United States Supreme Court called two New Deal programs, the National Recovery Act, and the Agricultural Adjustment Administration unconstitutional, cries were raised for a national constitutional convention.

After the Constitution was adopted, everything had to be tested for the first time. The provision in Article V which requires the Congress to convene a constitutional convention upon the call of two-thirds of the state legislatures is the only part of the Constitution that has not been tried. Some fear of the potential for mischief in convening a new constitutional convention is not surprising. The framers wrote the procedure for amending the Constitution as an afterthought, and its provisions were not as widely debated as other articles. We are the inheritors of the ambiguities of the Constitution. However, it should not be beyond the abilities of scholars, legislators, jurists, and political scientists to resolve the unanswered questions surrounding the call to take advantage of the opportunities while limiting the risks in another constitutional convention. And the American people have the common sense to make good choices. Should two-thirds of the state legislatures petition Congress for a convention, Congress will have to comply. In 1967, Senator Sam Ervin, a Democrat from North Carolina, proposed legislation to establish procedures for calling and running a convention to amend the Constitution. The legislation failed to pass more than once. Yet Congress ought to prepare for the possibility of calls for a convention and indeed for a new constitution, that are sometimes insistent and sometimes faint, but never entirely fade away.

Rexford Tugwell believed that the work of the Constitution's framers was essentially unfinished in that while the Constitution was " . . . framed by learned men . . . it was framed by men whose learning was soon to be discarded and overwhelmed by the century of discovery that was to follow. They cannot be blamed for not anticipating what was still totally hidden from them. This, however, does not excuse men of later generations who accepted their work as finished and failed to carry it forward."[20]

WE NEED A NEW CONSTITUTION

He could, of course, point to changes in the nation that the Founding Fathers could not even begin to imagine:

- *According to the Constitution a census or count of the people is taken every ten years. In 1790, when the first census was completed, the population of the United States was found to be 3.9 million. Today the resident population is about 250 million.*
- *When the Constitution was drafted, America was largely a rural nation. Boston and Philadelphia were the only cities with more than 25,000 people.*

Today, 77 percent of the population lives in metropolitan areas.

- *The America of the eighteenth century was mainly agrarian (farming), today's America is mainly industrial.*
- *In the eighteenth century, America was largely insulated from world affairs; today the nation is at the very center of global concerns.*
- *When the Constitution was written, the North American continent was largely unexplored and natural resources seemed inexhaustible. In the late twentieth century, available resources must be conserved.*
- *The Founding Fathers could give scant attention to air, water, and soil pollution, to toxic waste, global warming, or the depletion of the ozone layer. Protecting the environment is a grave concern today.*
- *The writers of the Constitution could not contemplate a threat of nuclear weapons.*

The framers of the Constitution recognized that the nation would change, so they acknowledged the Constitution's essentially experimental nature. But Thomas Finletter believed, "We have reached the end of an experiment. . . ."[21] and a new constitution building upon the nation's 200 years of experience and its new circumstances requires a radically new constitution.

In his book, *The Deadlock of Democracy*,[22] the historian James MacGregor Burns, showed how a stalemate in government may develop when the president and a majority of Congress are of different parties. A Democrat majority in Congress may be reluctant to adopt what a Republican president proposes. While the legislation Congress passes, the president may veto. And so, reform languishes. While Burns did not urge a totally new constitution for America, he did identify a number of important structural changes that he felt were necessary. These included mainly strengthening the nation's political parties and paying for political campaigns out of public funds.[23]

Those who see the need for a new constitution point with dismay at the data on low-voter participation and the increasing loss of confidence in America's institutions. According to one estimate, only 38 percent of eligible voters are "core" or regular voters who can be counted on to vote in major national and state elections.[24]

The adoption in 1971 of Amendment XXVI extending the vote to eighteen-year-olds did not make very much of a difference, as the following data demonstrate:[25]

CANDIDATES	VOTER PARTICIPATION (PERCENTAGE OF VOTING-AGE POPULATION)
1972 McGovern/Nixon	55.2
1976 Carter/Ford	54.0
1980 Carter/Regan	54.0
1984 Mondale/Reagan	53.1
1988 Dukakis/Bush	50.1
1992 Bush/Clinton	55.0

One of the most comprehensive surveys of the level of political apathy, the National Election Study of the Center for Political Studies, University of Michigan, reveals that 12 percent of the population report signing a petition, 5 percent report contributing to a political candidate, 4 percent have sent a letter to a government official, and only 2 percent have demonstrated for a political cause."[26] On the basis of these and related data the author concludes that " . . . the public is profoundly uninterested in the political world."[27]

Only 50 percent of those queried in a Gallup poll taken in 1991 had confidence in the American presidency; only 39 percent in the United States Supreme Court, and 18 percent in the Congress. "Fewer Americans today than at any time in the last two decades say they have a great deal or quite a lot of confidence in these institutions which . . . help form the foundation of American political life. . . . "[28]

A NEW CONSTITUTION IS NOT NEEDED

Justice Holmes wrote in *Abrams v. United States* (1919) "The Constitution is an experiment as all life is an experiment." In this light, all constitutional proposals remain experimental. It cannot be otherwise. The most distinguished scholars cannot anticipate unintended consequences that might come from their proposals. It is unlikely, barring a crisis that is perceived as threatening the very existence of the nation as did the crisis in 1787, that a consensus can develop around a totally new document. One person in the cloistered environment of a university can easily propose a new constitution. It is quite another matter to garner support for a new document in the hurly-burly of democratic politics where compromise reigns and many interests compete.

Currently, there is no consensus on the changes that are needed, or if any are needed at all. Moreover, no evidence indicates that proposed reforms would work better. Many incumbents fear losing the advantages they have under the current system. To them a constitutional convention, let alone a new constitution, is unthinkable.

A prominent political scientist, Norman J. Ornstein, insists that the Constitution does not need any fundamental change. "I think," he writes, "we will get through this period of searching and challenge; . . . with the system intact. I think that will happen because those who understand the political nature of the system, the importance of politics, the fundamental soundness of the system we have been given by the Founding Fathers will prevail. . . ."[29]

Adding to the dilemma is uncertainty; are political shortcomings caused by government structure or political leadership? The distinguished historian, James MacGregor Burns, believed it to be primarily a matter of government structure. The equally distinguished Arthur M. Schlesinger, Jr., is convinced that it is primarily the political leadership. He suggests that the media has so altered political parties and limited their functions that they are useless. Moreover, he writes, "New ideas have won access to politics through precisely those political crusaders who took the party away from the organization: TR (Theodore Roosevelt), (Woodrow) Wilson, FDR (Franklin Delano Roosevelt). The crusaders were responsive to needs and issues; the (political) bosses to habits and boodle."[30]

If divided government is a problem, nevertheless it has been the rule rather than the exception for most of the twentieth century. In his book, *Divided We Govern*, Professor David R. Mayhew demonstrates that 267 laws were enacted from 1947 through 1990. He concluded that divided partisan control between Congress and the White House makes "very little difference in the output of legislation."[31] The reason that government functions despite political divisions between Congress and the presidency is that both parties have defectors on one or more issues; sometimes Democrats vote with Republicans, and at other times Republicans vote with Democrats.

Voters, with their common sense, use divided government to prevent one branch from becoming too powerful. Writing in *The New York Times*, the ABC correspondent, Cokie Roberts, noted simply that we have divided government because "we like it." She continues, "They (voters) take the already formidable institutional checks and balances one step further by imposing a political check between the executive and legislative branches."[32]

There was more interest in the 1992 presidential election and higher voter turnout than in any election of the past twenty years. About 104 million Americans, or about 55 percent of those eligible, voted, ending a thirty-year decline in voter participation.[33] Led by Bill Clinton, the Democrats wrested the White House from the twelve-year lock held on it by Republicans. Well over one hundred new members were elected to Congress, including greater numbers of blacks, Hispanics, and women, making the legislative body more representative of the nation than in the past. With the Congress and the White House dominated by Democrats, divided government, in a political sense, does not exist. One party can make a difference in economic, political, and global matters, and reestablish confidence among Americans that their country is ready for the twenty-first century.

EPILOGUE

In this volume we have examined the pros and cons of a new American constitution and the arguments for and against convening a new constitutional convention. Do we need a new constitution and should a new constitutional convention be called to draft one? You will have to make up your own mind.

The political experiences of over 200 years serve to limit as well as to liberate. They liberate us if we have learned the right lessons of what practices in government to avoid and which to reform or even invent. They limit us because the roots of our history and the direction we have taken make it virtually impossible to alter course radically.

116

While some have proposed that Americans incorporate into their system aspects of the English parliamentary structure, it is highly unlikely that Americans would give up their system of checks and balances. Nor can it be expected that state boundaries will be altered.

It has been said that the only safeguard for democracy is more democracy, but a new constitution may not provide more democracy. It may, in fact, provide less. The Constitution of 1789 was not originally a democratic document. America became a democracy despite the Constitution not because of it. The Constitution was made a democratic instrument of government gradually through additions and changes. A Bill of Rights was added as a price for ratifying the Constitution. During the Progressive Era (1900–1920) the income tax (Amendment XVI), the direct election of Senators (Amendment XVII), and women's right to vote (Amendment XIX) were adopted. A Federal Reserve system strengthened the banking system, and anti-monopoly legislation was likewise advanced. At the state level voters gained the authority to propose legislation (initiative), to recall corrupt or ineffective lawmakers, and to hold referendums on laws passed by the legislature.

A nation does not need a constitution. Britain and Israel are parliamentary democracies in which there is no written constitution. America, too, can survive without a constitution, but tradition makes the Constitution the centerpiece of the political structure and the safeguard of freedoms. In 1888, in a speech to the Reform Club of New York, James Russell Lowell feared that Americans had come to view the Constitution "as a machine that would go of itself."[34] But the Constitution is not a machine and surely does not go of itself. It requires constant care and nurturing, adjusting, and fine tuning which a free people must provide.

If Americans sometimes appear apathetic, perhaps they have taken their freedoms for granted. When presidential arrogance led to attempts to short circuit the Constitution, as President Nixon did during the Vietnam era, the formidable, if clumsy, system of checks and balances contained the damage. In this country there has been no secret police, no KGB, no Gestapo, and no citizen has been subject to the chilling effect of secret police knocking on the door in the early hours of the morning.

This is not to say that this could not happen. We must be eternally vigilant. Thus far we have been lucky. For our luck to hold out requires us to take a detailed look at our Constitution and to make such midcourse corrections as the next millennium may require. What corrections should be made? Who will make them? How should they be made? Will you have the vision and the understanding to help make them?

NOTES

PROLOGUE
    1. Quoted in: Jeffrey Schmalz, "Americans are Sadder and Wiser, But Not Apathetic." *New York Times,* November 1, 1992.
    2. Quoted in: Dennis Farney "Even U.S. Politics Are Being Reshaped by a Global Economy." *Wall Street Journal,* October 28, 1992.

CHAPTER 1
    1. Samuel I. Rosenman, ed. *The Public Papers and Addresses of Franklin D. Roosevelt,* VI (New York, 1941) quoted in: Michael Kammen, ed. *The Origins of the American Constitution.* New York: Penguin Books, 1986, p. vii.
    2. Quoted in: Thomas H. Eliot, *Governing America: The Politics of a Free People.* New York: Dodd, Mead and Company, 1961, p. 39.
    3. "Observations on the New Constitution, and on the Federal and State Conventions. By a Columbian Patriot," Richard Henry Lee, ed. Quadrangle Books, 1962, pp. 1–19. Quoted in James MacGregor Burns, *The American Experiment: The Vineyard of Liberty.* New York: Alfred A. Knopf, 1982, p. 59.

4. Frank Monaghan, "Notes on the Inaugural Journey and the Inaugural Ceremonies of George Washington as First President of the United States." New York Public Library, 1939. Quoted in: *loc. cit.*, p. 67.
5. Roy P. Fairfield, ed. *The Federalist Papers,* No. 85. Garden City, New York: Doubleday and Company, Inc., Anchor Books, 1966, p. 272.
6. Michael Kammen, ed. *op. cit.*, p. xix.
7. Quoted in: Herbert Agar, *The Price of Union.* Boston: Houghton Mifflin Company, 1950, p. 40.
8. Richard Hofstadter, *The American Political Tradition.* New York: Vintage Books, 1989, p. 5.

CHAPTER 2
1. Roy P. Fairfield, ed. *The Federalist Papers.* Garden City, New York: Doubleday and Company, Inc., 1966, p. 115.
2. *Ibid.*, p. 26.
3. Quoted in: Max Lerner, *America as a Civilization.* New York: Simon and Schuster, 1957, p. 402.
4. *Ibid.*, p. 401.
5. Morton Grodzins, "Centralization and Decentralization in the American Federal System," in Robert A. Goldwin, ed. *A Nation of States.* Chicago: Rand McNally, 1951, pp. 1–23.
6. "State and Local Government Finances and Employment." *Statistical Abstract of the United States*, Washington, D.C.: United States Government Printing Office, 1991, p. 277.
7. Grodzins, *op. cit.*, p. 1.
8. Edward C. Banfield, *Here the People Rule.* New York: Plenum Press, 1985, p. 6.
9. New York: Warner Books, 1982, p. 102.
10. *Ibid.*
11. Quoted in: *Ibid.*
12. Daniel J. Elazar, "Opening the Third Century of American Federalism: Issues and Prospects." *Annals of the American Academy of Political and Social Science.* Vol. 509, May 1990, p. 112.

CHAPTER 3

1. Adam Clymer, "Public Believes Worst on Bank Scandal." *New York Times,* April 2, 1992, p. D21.

2. Roy P. Fairfield, ed. *The Federalist Papers* No. 51, Garden City, New York: Doubleday and Company, Inc., 1966, p. 160.

3. John Jay to George Washington, September 21, 1788. Quoted in: Michael Kammen, *Spheres of Liberty: Changing Concepts of Liberty in American Culture.* Madison, Wisconsin: University of Wisconsin Press, 1986, p. 12.

4. James Q. Wilson, "Does Separation of Powers Still Work?" *Public Interest.* Winter, 1987, p. 49.

5. These examples were drawn from: Nadine Cohodas, "Framers Make Conflict Between the Branches Part of the Natural Constitutional Order." *Congressional Quarterly Weekly Report,* Vol. 46, No. 2, July 2, 1988, pp. 1792–1793.

6. David R. Mayhew, *Divided We Govern: Party Control, Lawmaking, and Investigations, 1946–1990.* New Haven: Yale University Press, 1991, p. 4.

CHAPTER 4

1. Rich Jaroslovsky, "Political Alienation Shows Up in Pure Form in Nation's Nonvoters." *Wall Street Journal,* May 22, 1992, p. 1.

2. Mark S. Hoffman, ed. *The World Almanac and Book of Facts.* New York: Pharos Books, 1991, p. 383.

3. Cambridge, Massachusetts: Harvard University Press, 1990, pp. 1–2.

4. Henry Steele Commager, *Documents in American History.* Quoted in: James MacGregor Burns. *Cobblestone Leadership: Majority Rule, Minority Power.* Norman, Oklahoma: University of Oklahoma Press, 1990, p. 100.

5. James MacGregor Burns, *The Vineyard of Liberty.* New York: Alfred A. Knopf, 1982, p. 372.

6. David S. Broder, *The Party's Over: The Failure of Politics in America.* New York: Harper and Row Publishers, 1971, p. xxiii.

7. Gary R. Orren, "The Changing Styles of American

Party Politics" in James L. Lundquist, ed. *The Future of American Political Parties: The Challenge of Governance.* Englewood Cliffs, New Jersey: Prentice-Hall, Inc., 1982, p. 31.

8. James MacGregor Burns, *Cobblestone Leadership: Majority Rule, Minority Power. op. cit.,* p. 113.

9. Michael Wines, "President's Dinner Draws Donations, and Criticism," *New York Times,* April 27, 1992.

10. Herbert E. Alexander, 3rd Edition. *Financing Politics: Money, Elections and Political Reform.* Washington, D.C.: Congressional Quarterly Press, 1984, p. 5.

11. Data from: Herbert E. Alexander and Monica Bauer, *Financing the 1988 Election.* Boulder, Colorado: Westview Press Inc., 1991, pp. 1–2.

12. Elizabeth Kolbert, "Bypassing the Press Helps Candidates; Does it Also Serve the Public Interest?" *New York Times,* November 8, 1992.

13. Jill Abramson and Thomas Petzinger, Jr., "Big Political Donors Find Ways Around Watergate Reforms." *Wall Street Journal,* June 11, 1992, p. A. 12.

14. *New York Times,* June 7, 1992.

15. *New York Times Magazine,* June 14, 1992, p. 68.

CHAPTER 5

1. Quoted in: Haig A. Bosmajian, ed. *Freedom of Expression.* New York: Neal-Schuman, 1988, p. 5.

2. Roy P. Fairfield, ed. *The Federalist Papers,* No. 84. Garden City, New York: Doubleday and Company, Inc., Anchor Books, 1966, p. 263.

3. Ithiel de Sola Pool, *Technologies of Freedom.* Cambridge, Massachusetts: The Belknap Press of Harvard University, 1983, p. 10.

4. Franklin D. Roosevelt, *State of the Union Message.* 90 Congressional Record 57, 78th Congress, 2nd Session, January 11, 1944.

5. Quoted in: Dennis Farney, "As America Triumphs, Americans are Awash in Doubt and Pessimism." *Wall Street Journal,* July 27, 1992, p. 1.

6. Louis Henkin, "Constitutionalism and Human Rights." Louis Henkin and Albert J. Rosenthal, eds. *Con-*

stitutionalism and Rights. New York: Columbia University Press, 1990, p. 384.

CHAPTER 6

1. Quoted in: W. Russell Neuman, *The Paradox of Mass Politics: Knowledge and Opinion in the American Electorate.* Cambridge, Massachusetts: Harvard University Press, 1981, pp. 27–28.

2. Quoted in: Norman Ornstein, "The State of the Constitution," in Ralph S. Pollock, ed. *Renewing the Dream: Bicentennial Lectures on Contemporary Constitutional Issues.* New York: University Press of America, 1986, p. 132.

3. Paul J. Weber and Barbara A. Perry, *Unfounded Fears: Myths and Realities of a Constitutional Convention.* New York: Greenwood Press, 1989, pp. 81–82.

4. John R. Vile, *Rewriting the United States Constitution: An Examination of Proposals from Reconstruction to the Present.* New York: Praeger, 1991, p. 10.

5. New Rochelle, New York: Arlington House, Expanded version 1974, original 1942.

6. Thomas K. Finletter, *Can Representative Government Do the Job?* New York: Reynal and Hitchcock, 1945, p. 6.

7. Leland Baldwin, *Reforming the Constitution: An Imperative for Modern America.* Santa Barbara, California: Clio Press, 1972, p. xii.

8. *Ibid.*

9. Charles M. Hardin, *Presidential Power and Accountability: Toward a New Constitution.* Chicago: University of Chicago Press, 1974.

10. Rexford Tugwell, *The Emerging Constitution.* New York: Harper Magazine Press, 1974.

11. V.O. Key, *The Responsible Electorate.* New York: Vintage Books, 1966, p. 3.

12. *Ibid.,* p. 7.

13. "Ten Years of Public Opinion: An Ambivalent Public." *Public Opinion.* September/October, 1988, Vol. 11, No. 3, p. 4.

14. Quoted in: *Ibid.*

15. Quoted in: Richard Rovere, "Affairs of State." *New Yorker,* March 19, 1979, p. 137.

16. "Time for a People's Convention." *The Nation*, January 27, 1992, Vol. 254, No. 3, p. 94.

17. Rovere, *loc. cit.*

18. Boston: Little Brown and Company, 1966.

19. Quoted in: Paul J. Weber and Barbara A. Perry, *Unfounded Fears: Myths and Realities of a Constitutional Convention*. New York: Greenwood Press, 1989, p. 56.

20. Tugwell, *op. cit.*, p. 531.

21. Finletter, *op. cit.*, pp. 64–65.

22. Englewood Cliffs, New Jersey: Prentice-Hall Inc., 1963.

23. See James MacGregor Burns, *Cobblestone Leadership*. Norman, Oklahoma: University of Oklahoma Press, 1990, pp. 93–137.

24. Data from: James Reichley, ed. *Elections American Style*. Washington, D.C.: Brookings Institution, 1987, pp. 97–98.

25. Source: *The World Almanac and Book of Facts*. New York: Pharos Books, 1992, p. 426.

26. Quoted in: Neuman, *loc. cit.*, p. 11.

27. *Ibid.*, p. 9.

28. George Gallup and Dr. Frank Newport, "Confidence in Major U.S. Institutions at an All-time Low." *The Gallup Poll Monthly*, October, 1991, No. 313, p. 36.

29. Norman J. Ornstein, *op. cit.*, 140.

30. Arthur M. Schlesinger, Jr., "Can the Party System be Saved?" in Patricia Bonomi, James MacGregor Burns, Austin Ranney, eds. *The American Constitutional System Under Strong and Weak Parties*. New York: Praeger, 1981, p. 121.

31. New Haven: Yale University Press, 1991.

32. "Divided Government is the Best Revenge," p. A23.

33. *New York Times*, November 5, 1992.

34. Quoted in Michael Kammen, *A Machine that Would Go of Itself*. New York: Alfred A. Knopf, 1986, p. 18.

GLOSSARY

Amendment—a formal addition to the Constitution. Proposed by two-thirds vote of each house of Congress or by a national convention called by Congress at the request of two-thirds of the state legislatures. It needs to be ratified by the legislatures of three-fourths of the states or by conventions held in three-fourths of the states.

Appellate jurisdiction—authority of a court that hears appeals from lower courts.

Bicameral—a law-making body (legislature) which is made up of two houses. The United States Congress, with a House of Representatives and a Senate is bicameral.

Bill of attainder—a law convicting an individual or individuals of a particular crime and imposing a sentence without benefit of trial. For example, a law requiring blue-eyed men to pay a fine.

Bill of Rights—the first ten amendments to the United States Constitution, which guarantees the people their basic civil rights and liberties.

Cabinet—heads of executive departments who are appointed by the president. The president's cabinet now numbers fourteen.

Census—the official count of the nation's people authorized by the United States Constitution.

Checks and balances—the branches of the federal government restrain each other because each has different powers, terms, and requirements of office.

Concurrent powers—those powers shared by both the federal government and by the states.

Confederation—a form of government in which the parts (i.e. states, provinces, etc.) have greater authority than the central government.

Confirmation—as required by the Constitution, the Senate must approve treaties with foreign nations and certain presidential appointments.

Divided government—a condition that prevails when the president is of one party and a majority of the Congress is of another.

Division of powers—the sharing of powers between the states and the nation as in a federal system.

Dual citizenship—in the United States one is a citizen of the nation and of the state in which one lives.

Due process of law—fair legal procedures, a fair trial, as guaranteed mainly by Amendments V, VI, VII, VIII, and XIV.

Elastic clause—the "necessary and proper" clause found in Article I, Section 8 of the Constitution.

Electoral college—as required by the Constitution, voters do not vote directly for the president and vice president but for electors who initially were to have the power to make independent choices, but today they nearly always carry out the wishes of the voters.

Executive branch—the office of the president charged with the responsibility of administering the laws.

Ex post facto law—a law that penalizes an act that was not illegal at the time it was committed.

Expressed powers—also called delegated or enumerated powers of Congress, are listed in Article I, Section 8 of the United States Constitution.

Federal system—a form of government in which power is shared between a central government and its parts, that is, states, provinces, etc. Supreme power is vested in the former.

Filibuster—the power of Senators to block the passage of a bill through unlimited debate.

Full faith and credit clause—Article IV, Section 1 of the Constitution which requires that contracts, wills, etc. made in one state are legal in all other states.

Habeas corpus—"You shall have the body." A writ or court order, requiring an investigation into the reasons a prisoner is being held.

Impeachment—a trial in which, in the case of the president, the House brings the charges and the Senate acts as jury. Removal from office follows conviction. The president, vice president, and all civil officers of the United States may be impeached only for treason, bribery, or other high crimes and misdemeanors.

Implied powers—powers derived from expressed powers and the elastic clause of Article I, Section 8 of the Constitution. Given important expression in 1819 by Chief Justice John Marshall in *McCulloch v. Maryland*.

Independent regulatory commission—an agency created by Congress having partly legislative and judicial functions but operating out of the executive branch. Regulations regarding air travel, pure food and drugs, interstate transportation and communication are examples.

Initiative—a device enabling voters to introduce legislation by obtaining a certain number of signatures on a petition.

Injunction—a court order, a writ prohibiting a person from doing certain acts (e.g. picketing, demonstrating without a permit).

Interstate commerce—buying and selling of goods and services between the states or with foreign nations. Congress has jurisdiction.

Intrastate commerce—buying and selling of goods and services within a state.

Judicial activism—the tendency of the courts to impose their own social views on legislatures.

Judicial review—the power of a court to determine the constitutionality of a law on which a case brought before it is based.

Judicial self-restraint—the Supreme Court will limit its views to the constitutionality of the law. The opposite of judicial self-restraint is judicial activism.

Judiciary—that branch of government that interprets the laws. The United States Supreme Court and lesser federal and state courts.

Jury—a group of people, usually six in a civil suit, twelve in a criminal case, who are called upon to decide if a person brought before the court is guilty as charged or innocent. A grand jury, usually of twenty-four, determines whether or not there is enough evidence to bring charges.

Lame duck—an office holder that has not been elected but continues in office until the expiration of the term.

Legislature—the law-making body. In the United States it is the Congress. Each state has its own law-making body.

Lower house—usually the larger and more representative body in a bicameral legislature. In the Congress it is the House of Representatives.

Original jurisdiction—the authority of a court to hear cases before other courts.

PAC—Political Action Committees representing special interests such as people in a common profession (e.g. lawyers), or those seeking to reform Congress as Common Cause, or those seeking to promote or defeat specific legislation as the National Rifle Association (NRA), which opposes gun control.

Pocket veto—the refusal of the president to sign a bill by holding it for ten days during which time Congress adjourns.

Police powers—the powers of state or federal government to regulate the health and safety of its citizens.

Poll tax—a direct tax levied by local governments on all adults. Often used as a requirement for voting but made illegal by Amendment XXIV (1964).

Preamble—technically not a part of the Constitution, it "walks before" and sets out its purposes.

Privileges and immunities clause—Article IV, Section 2 which provides that the people of one state may enjoy the same rights as the people of another state.

Republic—a nation that has no king and in which elected representatives govern.

Residual powers—are powers which are not given to the federal government and not denied the states, and so are reserved to the states.

Separation of powers—the distribution of powers among the legislative, executive, and judicial branches of government so that one branch does not become too powerful. Makes checks and balances possible.

Spoils system—the power of the victorious candidate or party to reward political followers by appointing them to office.

Statute—a law passed by a legislative body.

Strict construction—the philosophy that would strictly limit the authority of government by taking a very narrow interpretation of the Constitution.

Suffrage—the right to vote in an election.

129

Unicameral—a legislature of one house.

Unwritten constitution—made up of customs, practices, traditions, laws, and court decisions, which are not included in the Constitution—the supreme law of the land.

Upper house—usually the smaller house. In the Congress it is the Senate in which there are 100 members, two from each state.

Veto—the refusal of the president to sign a bill passed by Congress.

War powers resolution—passed by Congress in 1973 in the aftermath of the Vietnam War to place limits on the president's war-making powers.

Written constitution—a single document drawn up at one time to be the fundamental law upon which a government is based and according to which it functions.

FOR FURTHER READING

Alexander, Herbert E. *Financing Politics: Money, Elections, and Political Reform*. Washington, D.C.: Congressional Quarterly Press, 1984.

Bowen, Catherine Drinker. *Miracle at Philadelphia: The Story of the Constitutional Convention, May to September, 1787*. Boston: Little Brown and Company, 1986.

Broder, David S. *The Party's Over: The Failure of Politics in America*. New York: Harper and Row Publishers, 1971.

Burns, James MacGregor and Stewart Burns. *A People's Charter: The Pursuit of Rights in America*. New York: Alfred A. Knopf, 1991.

Burns, James MacGregor. *Deadlock of Democracy: Four Party Politics in America*. Englewood Cliffs, New Jersey: Prentice-Hall, Inc., 1963.

Fairfield, Roy P., ed. *The Federalist Papers*. Garden City, New York: Doubleday and Company, Inc., Anchor Books, 1966.

Friendly, Fred W. and Martha Eliot. *The Constitution: That Delicate Balance*. New York: Random House, 1984.

Henkin, Louis. *The Age of Rights*. New York: Columbia University Press, 1990.

Kammen, Michael, ed. *The Origins of the American Constitution*. New York: Penguin Books, 1986.

Mayhew, David R. *Divided We Govern*. New Haven: Yale University Press, 1991.

Poole, Ithiel de Sola. *Technologies of Freedom*. Cambridge, Massachusetts: The Belknap Press of Harvard University, 1983.

Sundquist, James L. *Constitutional Reform and Effective Government*. Washington, D.C.: The Brookings Institute, 1986.

Will, George. *Restoration. Congress, Term Limits and the Recovery of Deliberative Democracy*. New York: The Free Press, 1992.

APPENDIX A:
CONSTITUTIONAL SEPARATION OF POWERS

FEDERAL GOVERNMENT   STATES

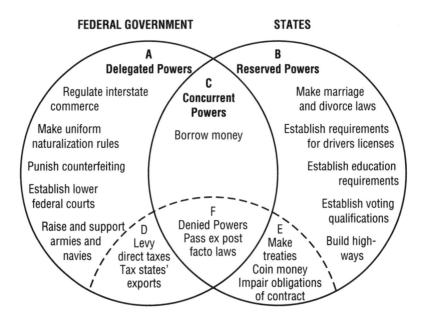

A
Delegated Powers

Regulate interstate commerce

Make uniform naturalization rules

Punish counterfeiting

Establish lower federal courts

Raise and support armies and navies

B
Reserved Powers

Make marriage and divorce laws

Establish requirements for drivers licenses

Establish education requirements

Establish voting qualifications

Build highways

C
Concurrent Powers

Borrow money

D
Levy direct taxes

Tax states' exports

F
Denied Powers
Pass ex post facto laws

E
Make treaties

Coin money

Impair obligations of contract

APPENDIX B:
CONSTITUTION OF THE UNITED STATES

We the People of the United States, in Order to form a more perfect Union, establish Justice, insure domestic Tranquility, provide for the common defense, promote the general Welfare, and secure the Blessings of Liberty to ourselves and our Posterity, do ordain and establish this Constitution for the United States of America.

ARTICLE. I.

SECTION. 1. All legislative Powers herein granted shall be vested in a Congress of the United States, which shall consist of a Senate and House of Representatives.

SECTION. 2. The House of Representatives shall be composed of Members chosen every second Year by the People of the several States, and the Electors in each State shall have the Qualifications requisite for Electors of the most numerous Branch of the State Legislature.

No Person shall be a Representative who shall not have attained to the age of twenty five Years, and been seven Years a Citizen of the United States, and who shall not, when elected, be an Inhabitant of that State in which he shall be chosen.

Representatives and direct Taxes shall be apportioned among the several States which may be included within this Union, according to their respective Numbers, which shall be determined by adding to the whole Number of free Persons, including those bound to Service for a Term of Years, and excluding Indians not taxed, three fifths of all other Persons. The actual Enumeration shall be made within three Years after the first Meeting of the Congress of the United States, and within every subsequent Term of ten Years, in such Manner as they shall by Law direct. The Number of Representatives shall not exceed one for every thirty Thousand, but each State shall have at Least one Representative; and until such enumeration shall be made, the State of New Hampshire shall be entitled to chuse three, Massachusetts eight, Rhode-Island and Providence Plantations one, Connecticut five, New-York six, New Jersey four, Pennsylvania eight, Delaware one, Maryland six, Virginia ten, North Carolina five, South Carolina five, and Georgia three.

When vacancies happen in the Representation from any State, the Executive Authority thereof shall issue Writs of Election to fill such Vacancies.

The House of Representatives shall chuse their Speaker and other Officers; and shall have the sole Power of Impeachment.

SECTION. 3. The Senate of the United States shall be composed of two Senators from each State, chosen by the Legislature thereof, for six Years; and each Senator shall have one Vote.

Immediately after they shall be assembled in Consequence of the first Election, they shall be divided as equally as may be into three Classes. The Seats of the Senators of the first Class shall be vacated at the Expiration of the second Year, of the second Class at the Expiration of the fourth Year, and of the third Class at the Expiration of the sixth Year, so that one third may be chosen every second Year; and if Vacancies happen by Resignation, or otherwise, during the Recess of the Legislature of any State, the Executive thereof may make temporary Appointments until the next Meeting of the Legislature, which shall then fill such Vacancies.

No Person shall be a Senator who shall not have attained to the Age of thirty Years, and been nine Years a Citizen of the United States, and who shall not, when elected, be an Inhabitant of that State for which he shall be chosen.

The Vice President of the United States shall be President of the Senate, but shall have no Vote, unless they be equally divided.

The Senate shall chuse their other Officers, and also a President pro tempore, in the Absence of the Vice President, or when he shall exercise the Office of President of the United States.

The Senate shall have the sole Power to try all Impeachments. When sitting for that Purpose, they shall be on Oath or Affirmation. When the President of the United States is tried the Chief Justice shall preside: And no Person shall be convicted without the Concurrence of two thirds of the Members present.

Judgment in Cases of Impeachment shall not extend further than to removal from Office, and disqualification to hold and enjoy any Office of honor, Trust or Profit under the United States: but the Party convicted shall nevertheless be liable and subject to

Indictment, Trial, Judgment and Punishment, according to Law.

SECTION. 4. The Times, Places and Manner of holding Elections for Senators and Representatives, shall be prescribed in each State by the Legislature thereof; but the Congress may at any time by Law make or alter such Regulations, except as to the Places of chusing Senators.

The Congress shall assemble at least once in every Year, and such Meeting shall be on the first Monday in December, unless they shall by Law appoint a different Day.

SECTION. 5. Each House shall be the Judge of the Elections, Returns and Qualifications of its own Members, and a Majority of each shall constitute a Quorum to do Business; but a smaller Number may adjourn from day to day, and may be authorized to compel the Attendance of absent Members, in such Manner, and under such Penalties as each House may provide.

Each House may determine the Rules of its Proceedings, punish its Members for disorderly Behaviour, and, with the Concurrence of two thirds, expel a Member.

Each House shall keep a Journal of its Proceedings, and from time to time publish the same, excepting such Parts as may in their Judgment require Secrecy; and the Yeas and Nays of the Members of either House on any question shall, at the Desire of one fifth of those Present, be entered on the Journal.

Neither House, during the Session of Congress, shall, without the Consent of the other, adjourn for more than three days, nor to any other Place than that in which the two Houses shall be sitting.

SECTION. 6. The Senators and Representatives shall receive a Compensation for their Services, to be ascertained by Law, and paid out of the Treasury of the United States. They shall in all Cases, except Treason, Felony and Breach of the Peace, be privileged from Arrest during their Attendance at the Session of their respective Houses, and in going to and returning from the same; and for any Speech or Debate in either House, they shall not be questioned in any other Place.

No Senator or Representative shall, during the Time for which he was elected, be appointed to any civil Office under the Authority of the United States, which shall have been created, or the Emoluments whereof shall have been encreased during such time; and no Person holding any Office under the United States, shall be a Member of either House during his Continuance in Office.

SECTION. 7. All Bills for raising Revenue shall originate in the House of Representatives; but the Senate may propose or concur with amendments as on other Bills.

Every Bill which shall have passed the House of Representatives and the Senate, shall, before it become a Law, be presented to the President of the United States; If he approve he shall sign it, but if not he shall return it, with his Objections to that House in which it shall have originated, who shall enter the Objections at large on their Journal, and proceed to reconsider it. If after such Reconsideration two thirds of that House shall agree to pass the Bill, it shall be sent, together with the Objections, to the other House, by which it shall likewise be reconsidered, and if approved by two thirds of that House, it shall become a Law. But in all such Cases the Votes of both Houses shall be determined by yeas and Nays, and the Names of the Persons voting for and against the Bill shall be entered on the Journal of each House respectively. If any Bill shall not be returned by the President within ten Days (Sundays excepted) after it shall have been presented to him, the Same shall be a Law, in like Manner as if he had signed it, unless the Congress by their Adjournment prevent its Return, in which Case it shall not be a Law.

Every Order, Resolution, or Vote to which the Concurrence of the Senate and House of Representatives may be necessary (except on a question of Adjournment) shall be presented to the President of the United States; and before the Same shall take Effect, shall be approved by him, or being disapproved by him, shall be repassed by two thirds of the Senate and House of Representatives, according to the Rules and Limitations prescribed in the Case of a Bill.

SECTION. 8. The Congress shall have Power To lay and collect Taxes, Duties, Imposts and Excises, to pay the Debts and provide for the common Defence and general Welfare of the United States; but all Duties, Imposts and Excises shall be uniform throughout the United States;

To borrow Money on the credit of the United States;

To regulate Commerce with foreign Nations, and among the several States, and with the Indian Tribes;

To establish an uniform Rule of Naturalization, and uniform Laws on the subject of Bankruptcies throughout the United States;

To coin Money, regulate the Value thereof, and of foreign Coin, and fix the Standard of Weights and Measures;

To provide for the Punishment of counterfeiting the Securities and current Coin of the United States;

To establish Post Offices and post Roads;

To promote the Progress of Science and useful Arts, by securing for limited Times to Authors and Inventors the exclusive Right to their respective Writings and Discoveries;

To constitute Tribunals inferior to the supreme Court;

To define and punish Piracies and Felonies committed on the high Seas, and offences against the Law of Nations;

To declare War, grant Letters of Marque and Reprisal, and make Rules concerning Captures on Land and Water;

To raise and support Armies, but no Appropriation of Money to that Use shall be for a longer Term than two Years;

To provide and maintain a Navy;

To make Rules for the Government and Regulation of the land and naval Forces;

To provide for calling forth the Militia to execute the Laws of the Union, suppress Insurrections and repel Invasions;

To provide for organizing, arming, and disciplining, the Militia, and for governing such Part of them as may be employed in the Service of the United States, reserving to the States respectively, the Appointment of the Officers, and the Authority of training the Militia according to the discipline prescribed by Congress;

To exercise exclusive Legislation in all Cases whatsoever, over such District (not exceeding ten Miles square) as may, by Cession of Particular States, and the Acceptance of Congress, become the Seat of the Government of the United States, and to exercise like Authority over all Places purchased by the Consent of the Legislature of the State in which the Same shall be, for the Erection of Forts, Magazines, Arsenals, dock-Yards, and other needful Buildings;—And

To make all Laws which shall be necessary and proper for carrying into Execution the foregoing Powers, and all other Powers vested by this Constitution in the Government of the United States, or in any Department or Officer thereof.

SECTION. 9. The Migration or Importation of such Persons as any of the States now existing shall think proper to admit, shall not be prohibited by the Congress prior to the Year one thousand eight hundred and eight, but a Tax or duty may be imposed on such Importation, not exceeding ten dollars for each Person.

The Privilege of the Writ of Habeas Corpus shall not be suspended, unless when in Cases of Rebellion or Invasion the public Safety may require it.

No Bill of Attainder or ex post facto Law shall be passed.

No Capitation, or other direct, Tax shall be laid, unless in Proportion to the Census or Enumeration herein before directed to be taken.

No Tax or Duty shall be laid on Articles exported from any State.

No Preference shall be given by any Regulation of Commerce or Revenue to the Ports of one State over those of another; nor shall Vessels bound to, or from, one State, be obliged to enter, clear or pay Duties in another.

No Money shall be drawn from the Treasury, but in Consequence of Appropriations made by Law; and a regular Statement and Account of the Receipts and Expenditures of all public Money shall be published from time to time.

No Title of Nobility shall be granted by the United States: And no Person holding any Office of Profit or Trust under them, shall, without the Consent of the Congress, accept of any present, Emolument, Office, or Title, of any kind whatever, from any King, Prince, or foreign State.

SECTION. 10. No State shall enter into any Treaty, Alliance, or Confederation; grant Letters of Marque and Reprisal; coin Money; emit Bills of Credit; make any Thing but gold and silver Coin a Tender in Payment of Debts; pass any Bill of Attainder, ex post facto Law, or Law impairing the Obligation of Contracts, or grant any Title of Nobility.

No State shall, without the Consent of the Congress, lay any Imposts or Duties on Imports or Exports, except what may be absolutely necessary for executing its inspection Laws: and the net Produce of all Duties and Imposts, laid by any State on Imports or Exports, shall be for the Use of the Treasury of the United States; and all such Laws shall be subject to the Revision and Controul of the Congress.

No State shall, without the Consent of Congress, lay any Duty of Tonnage, keep Troops, or Ships of War in time of Peace, enter into any Agreement or Compact with another State, or with a foreign Power, or engage in War, unless actually invaded, or in such imminent Danger as will not admit of delay.

ARTICLE. II.

SECTION. 1. The executive Power shall be vested in a President of the United States of America. He shall hold his Office during the Term of four Years, and, together with the Vice President, chosen for the same Term, be elected, as follows

Each State shall appoint, in such Manner as the Legislature thereof may direct, a Number of Electors, equal to the whole Number of Senators and Representatives to which the State may be entitled in the Congress: but no Senator or Representative, or Person holding an office of Trust or Profit under the United States, shall be appointed an Elector.

The Electors shall meet in their respective States, and vote by Ballot for Two Persons, of whom one at least shall not be an Inhabitant of the same State with themselves. And they shall make a List of all the Persons voted for, and of the Number of Votes for each; which List they shall sign and certify, and transmit sealed to the Seat of the Government of the United States, directed to the President of the Senate. The

President of the Senate shall, in the Presence of the Senate and House of Representatives, open all the Certificates, and the Votes shall then be counted. The Person having the greatest Number of Votes shall be the President, if such Number be a Majority of the whole Number of Electors appointed; and if there be more than one who have such Majority, and have an equal Number of Votes, then the House of Representatives shall immediately chuse by Ballot one of them for President; and if no Person have a Majority, then from the five highest on the List the said House shall in like Manner chuse the President. But in chusing the President, the Votes shall be taken by States, the Representation from each State having one Vote; a quorum for this Purpose shall consist of a Member or Members from two thirds of the States, and a Majority of all the States shall be necessary to a Choice. In every Case, after the Choice of the President, the Person having the greatest Number of Votes of the Electors shall be the Vice President. But if there should remain two or more who have equal Votes, the Senate shall chuse from them by Ballot the Vice President.

The Congress may determine the Time of chusing the Electors, and the Day on which they shall give their Votes; which Day shall be the same throughout the United States.

No Person except a natural born Citizen, or a Citizen of the United States, at the time of the Adoption of this Constitution, shall be eligible to the Office of President; neither shall any person be eligible to that Office who shall not have attained to the Age of thirty five Years, and been fourteen Years a Resident within the United States.

In Case of the Removal of the President from Office, or of his Death, Resignation, or Inability to discharge the Powers and Duties of the said Office, the Same shall devolve on the Vice President, and the Congress may by Law provide for the Case of Removal, Death, Resignation or Inability, both of the President and Vice President, declaring what Officer shall then act as President, and such Officer shall act accordingly, until the Disability be removed, or a President shall be elected.

The President shall, at stated Times, receive for his Services, a Compensation, which shall neither be increased nor diminished during the Period for which he shall have been elected, and he shall not receive within that period any other Emolument from the United States, or any of them.

Before he enter on the Execution of his Office, he shall take the following Oath or Affirmation:—"I do solemnly swear (or affirm) that I will faithfully execute the Office of President of the United States, and will to the best of my Ability, preserve, protect and defend the Constitution of the United States."

SECTION. 2. The President shall be Commander in Chief of the Army and Navy of the United States, and of the Militia of the several States, when called into the actual Service of the United States; he may require the Opinion, in writing, of the principal Officer in each of the executive Departments, upon any Subject relating to the Duties of their respective Offices, and he shall have Power to grant Reprieves and Pardons for Offences against the United States, except in Cases of Impeachment.

He shall have Power, by and with the Advice and Consent of the Senate, to make Treaties, provided two thirds of the Senators present concur; and he shall nominate, and by and with the Advice and Consent of the Senate, shall appoint Ambassadors, other public Ministers and Consuls, Judges of the supreme Court, and all other Officers of the United States, whose Appointments are not herein otherwise provided for, and which shall be established by Law: but the Congress may by Law vest the Appointment of such inferior Officers, as they think proper, in the President alone, in the Courts of Law, or in the Heads of Departments.

The President shall have Power to fill up all Vacancies that may happen during the Recess of the Senate, by granting Commissions which shall expire at the End of their next Session.

SECTION. 3. He shall from time to time give to the Congress Information of the State of the Union, and recommend to their Consideration such Measures as he shall judge necessary and expedient; he may, on extraordinary Occasions, convene both Houses, or either of them, and in Case of Disagreement between them, with Respect to the Time of Adjournment, he may adjourn them to such Time as he shall think proper; he shall receive Ambassadors and other public Ministers; he shall take Care that the Laws be faithfully executed, and shall Commission all the Officers of the United States.

SECTION. 4. The President, Vice President and all civil Officers of the United States, shall be removed from Office on Impeachment for, and Conviction of, Treason, Bribery, or other high Crimes and Misdemeanors.

ARTICLE. III.

SECTION. 1. The judicial Power of the United States, shall be vested in one supreme Court, and in such inferior Courts as the Congress may from time to time ordain and establish. The Judges, both of the supreme and inferior Courts, shall hold their Offices during good Behaviour, and shall, at stated Times, receive for their Services, a Compensation, which shall not be diminished during their Continuance in Office.

SECTION. 2. The judicial Power shall extend to

all Cases, in Law and Equity, arising under this Constitution, the Laws of the United States, and Treaties made, or which shall be made, under their Authority;—to all Cases affecting Ambassadors, other public Ministers and Consuls;—to all Cases of admiralty and maritime Jurisdiction;—to Controversies to which the United States shall be a Party;—to Controversies between two or more States;—between a State and Citizens of another State;—between Citizens of different States;—between Citizens of the same State claiming Lands under Grants of different States, and between a State, or the Citizens thereof, and foreign States, Citizens or Subjects.

In all Cases affecting Ambassadors, other public Ministers and Consuls, and those in which a State shall be Party, the supreme Court shall have original Jurisdiction. In all the other Cases before mentioned, the supreme Court shall have appellate Jurisdiction, both as to Law and Fact, with such Exceptions, and under such Regulations as the Congress shall make.

The Trial of all Crimes, except in Cases of Impeachment, shall be by Jury; and such Trial shall be held in the State where the said Crimes shall have been committed; but when not committed within any State, the Trial shall be at such Place and or Places as the Congress may by Law have directed.

Section. 3. Treason against the United States, shall consist only in levying War against them, or in adhering to their Enemies, giving them Aid and Comfort. No Person shall be convicted of Treason unless on the Testimony of two Witnesses to the same overt Act, or on Confession in open Court.

The Congress shall have Power to declare the Punishment of Treason, but no Attainder of Treason shall work Corruption of Blood, or Forfeiture except during the Life of the Person attainted.

ARTICLE. IV.

Section. 1. Full Faith and Credit shall be given in each State to the public Acts, Records, and judicial Proceedings of every other State. And the Congress may by general Laws prescribe the Manner in which such Acts, Records and Proceedings shall be proved, and the Effect thereof.

Section. 2. The Citizens of each State shall be entitled to all Privileges and Immunities of Citizens in the several States.

A Person charged in any State with Treason, Felony, or other Crime, who shall flee from Justice, and be found in another State, shall on Demand of the executive Authority of the State from which he fled, be delivered up, to be removed to the State having Jurisdiction of the Crime.

No Person held to Service or Labour in one State, under the Laws thereof, escaping into another, shall, in Consequence of any Law or Regulation therein, be discharged from such Service or Labour, but shall be delivered up on Claim of the Party to whom such Service or Labour may be due.

Section. 3. New States may be admitted by the Congress into this Union; but no new State shall be formed or erected within the Jurisdiction of any other State; nor any State be formed by the Junction of two or more States, or Parts of States, without the Consent of the Legislatures of the States concerned as well as of the Congress.

The Congress shall have Power to dispose of and make all needful Rules and Regulations respecting the Territory or other Property belonging to the United States; and nothing in this Constitution shall be so construed as to Prejudice any Claims of the United States, or of any particular State.

Section. 4. The United States shall guarantee to every State in this Union a Republican Form of Government, and shall protect each of them against Invasion; and on Application of the Legislature, or of the Executive (when the Legislature cannot be convened) against domestic Violence.

ARTICLE. V.

The Congress, whenever two thirds of both Houses shall deem it necessary, shall propose Amendments to this Constitution, or, on the Application of the Legislatures of two thirds of the several States, shall call a Convention for proposing Amendments, which, in either Case, shall be valid to all Intents and Purposes, as Part of this Constitution, when ratified by the Legislatures of three fourths of the several States, or by Conventions in three fourths thereof, as the one or the other Mode of Ratification may be proposed by the Congress; Provided that no Amendment which may be made prior to the Year One thousand eight hundred and eight shall in any Manner affect the first and fourth Clauses in the Ninth Section of the first Article; and that no State, without its Consent, shall be deprived of its equal Suffrage in the Senate.

ARTICLE. VI.

All Debts contracted and Engagements entered into, before the Adoption of this Constitution, shall be as valid against the United States under this Constitution, as under the Confederation.

This Constitution, and the Laws of the United States which shall be made in Pursuance thereof; and all Treaties made, or which shall be made, under the Authority of the United States, shall be the supreme Law of the Land; and the Judges in every State shall be bound thereby, any Thing in the Constitution or Laws of any State to the Contrary notwithstanding.

The Senators and Representatives before Mentioned, and the Members of the several State Legislatures, and all executive and judicial Officers, both of the United States and of the several States, shall be bound by Oath or Affirmation, to support this Constitution; but no religious Test shall ever be required as a Qualification to any Office or public Trust under the United States.

ARTICLE VII.

The Ratification of the Conventions of nine States, shall be sufficient for the Establishment of this Constitution between the States so ratifying the same. Done in Convention by the Unanimous Consent of the States present the Seventeenth Day of September in the Year of our Lord one thousand seven hundred and Eighty seven and of the Independence of the United States of America the Twelfth In witness whereof We have hereunto subscribed our Names,

THE BILL OF RIGHTS

AMENDMENT I.

Congress shall make no law respecting an establishment of religion, or prohibiting the free exercise thereof; or abridging the freedom of speech, or of the press; or the right of the people peaceably to assemble, and to petition the Government for a redress of grievances.

AMENDMENT II.

A well regulated Militia, being necessary to the security of a free State, the right of the people to keep and bear Arms, shall not be infringed.

AMENDMENT III.

No Soldier shall, in time of peace be quartered in any house, without the consent of the Owner, nor in time of war, but in a manner to be prescribed by law.

AMENDMENT IV.

The right of the people to be secure in their persons, houses, papers, and effects, against unreasonable searches and seizures, shall not be violated, and no Warrants shall issue, but upon probable cause, supported by Oath or affirmation, and particularly describing the place to be searched, and the persons or things to be seized.

AMENDMENT V.

No person shall be held to answer for a capital, or otherwise infamous crime, unless on a presentment or indictment of a Grand Jury, except in cases arising in the land or naval forces, or in the Militia, when in actual service in time of War or public danger; nor shall any person be subject for the same offence to be twice put in jeopardy of life or limb; nor shall be compelled in any criminal case to be a wit-

ness against himself, nor be deprived of life, liberty, or property, without due process of law; nor shall private property be taken for public use, without just compensation.

AMENDMENT VI.

In all criminal prosecutions, the accused shall enjoy the right to a speedy and public trial, by an impartial jury of the State and district wherein the crime shall have been committed, which district shall have been previously ascertained by law, and to be informed of the nature and cause of the accusation; to be confronted with the witnesses against him; to have compulsory process for obtaining witnesses in his favor, and to have the Assistance of Counsel for his defence.

AMENDMENT VII.

In Suits at common law, where the value in controversy shall exceed twenty dollars, the right of trial by jury shall be preserved, and no fact tried by a jury, shall be otherwise re-examined in any Court of the United States, than according to the rules of the common law.

AMENDMENT VIII.

Excessive bail shall not be required, nor excessive fines imposed, nor cruel and unusual punishments inflicted.

AMENDMENT IX.

The enumeration in the Constitution, of certain rights, shall not be construed to deny or disparage others retained by the people.

AMENDMENT X.

The powers not delegated to the United States by the Constitution, nor prohibited by it to the States, are reserved to the States respectively, or to the people.

AMENDMENT XI.

The Judicial power of the United States shall not be construed to extend to any suit in law or equity, commenced or prosecuted against one of the United States by Citizens of another State, or by Citizens or Subjects of any Foreign State.

AMENDMENT XII.

The Electors shall meet in their respective states and vote by ballot for President and Vice-President, one of whom, at least, shall not be an inhabitant of the same state with themselves; they shall name in their ballots the person voted for as President, and in distinct ballots the person voted for as Vice-President, and they shall make distinct lists of all persons voted for as President, and of all persons voted for as Vice-

President, and of the number of votes for each, which lists they shall sign and certify, and transmit sealed to the seat of the government of the United States, directed to the President of the Senate;—The President of the Senate shall, in the presence of the Senate and House of Representatives, open all the certificates and the votes shall then be counted;—The person having the greatest number of votes for President, shall be the President, if such number be a majority of the whole number of Electors appointed; and if no person have such majority, then from the persons having the highest numbers not exceeding three on the list of those voted for as President, the House of Representatives shall choose immediately, by ballot, the President. But in choosing the President, the votes shall be taken by states, the representation from each state having one vote; a quorum for this purpose shall consist of a member or members from two-thirds of the states, and a majority of all the states shall be necessary to a choice. And if the House of Representatives shall not choose a President whenever the right of choice shall devolve upon them, before the fourth day of March next following, then the Vice-President shall act as President, as in the case of the death or other constitutional disability of the President—The person having the greatest number of votes as Vice-President, shall be the Vice-President, if such number be a majority of the whole number of Electors appointed, and if no person have a majority, then from the two highest numbers on the list, the Senate shall choose the Vice-President; a quorum for the purpose shall consist of two-thirds of the whole number of Senators, and a majority of the whole number shall be necessary to a choice. But no person constitutionally ineligible to the office of President shall be eligible to that of Vice-President of the United States.

AMENDMENT XIII.

SECTION 1. Neither slavery nor involuntary servitude, except as a punishment for crime whereof the party shall have been duly convicted, shall exist within the United States, or any place subject to their jurisdiction.

SECTION 2. Congress shall have power to enforce this article by appropriate legislation.

AMENDMENT XIV.

SECTION 1. All persons born or naturalized in the United States and subject to the jurisdiction thereof, are citizens of the United States and of the State wherein they reside. No State shall make or enforce any law which shall abridge the privileges or immunities of citizens of the United States; nor shall any State deprive any person of life, liberty, or property, without due process of law; nor deny to any person within its jurisdiction the equal protection of the laws.

SECTION 2. Representatives shall be apportioned among the several States according to their respective numbers, counting the whole number of persons in each State, excluding Indians not taxed. But when the right to vote at any election for the choice of electors for President and Vice President of the United States, Representatives in Congress, the Executive and Judicial officers of a State, or the members of the Legislature thereof, is denied to any of the male inhabitants of such State, being twenty-one years of age, and citizens of the United States, or in any way abridged, except for participation in rebellion, or other crime, the basis of representation therein shall be reduced in the proportion which the number of such male citizens shall bear to the whole number of male citizens twenty-one years of age in such State.

SECTION 3. No person shall be a Senator or Representative in Congress, or elector of President and Vice President, or hold any office, civil or military, under the United States, or under any State, who, having previously taken an oath, as a member of Congress, or as an officer of the United States, or as a member of any State legislature, or as an executive or judicial officer of any State, to support the Constitution of the United States, shall have engaged in insurrection or rebellion against the same, or given aid or comfort to the enemies thereof. But Congress may by a vote of two-thirds of each House, remove such disability.

SECTION 4. The validity of the public debt of the United States, authorized by law, including debts incurred for payment of pensions and bounties for services in suppressing insurrection or rebellion, shall not be questioned. But neither the United States nor any State shall assume or pay any debt or obligation incurred in aid of insurrection or rebellion against the United States, or any claim for the loss or emancipation of any slave; but all such debts, obligations and claims shall be held illegal and void.

SECTION 5. The Congress shall have power to enforce, by appropriate legislation, the provisions of this article.

AMENDMENT XV.

SECTION 1. The right of citizens of the United States to vote shall not be denied or abridged by the United States or by any State on account of race, color, or previous condition of servitude.

SECTION 2. The Congress shall have power to enforce this article by appropriate legislation.

AMENDMENT XVI.

The Congress shall have power to lay and collect taxes on incomes, from whatever source derived, without apportionment among the several States, and without regard to any census or enumeration.

AMENDMENT XVII.

The Senate of the United States shall be composed of two Senators from each State, elected by the people thereof, for six years; and each Senator shall have one vote. The electors in each State shall have the qualifications requisite for electors of the most numerous branch of the State legislatures.

When vacancies happen in the representation of any State in the Senate, the executive authority of such State shall issue writs of election to fill such vacancies: *Provided,* That the legislature of any State may empower the executive thereof to make temporary appointments until the people fill the vacancies by election as the legislature may direct.

This amendment shall not be so construed as to affect the election or term of any Senator chosen before it becomes valid as part of the Constitution.

AMENDMENT XVIII.

SECTION 1. After one year from the ratification of this article the manufacture, sale, or transportation of intoxicating liquors within, the importation thereof into, or the exportation thereof from the United States and all territory subject to the jurisdiction thereof for beverage purposes is hereby prohibited.

SECTION 2. The Congress and the several States shall have concurrent power to enforce this article by appropriate legislation.

SECTION 3. This article shall be inoperative unless it shall have been ratified as an amendment to the Constitution by the legislatures of the several States, as provided in the Constitution, within seven years from the date of the submission hereof to the States by the Congress.

AMENDMENT XIX.

The right of citizens of the United States to vote shall not be denied or abridged by the United States or by any State on account of sex.

Congress shall have power to enforce this article by appropriate legislation.

AMENDMENT XX.

SECTION 1. The terms of the President and Vice President shall end at noon on the 20th day of January, and the terms of Senators and Representatives at noon on the 3d day of January, of the years in which such terms would have ended if this article had not been ratified; and the terms of their successors shall then begin.

SECTION 2. The Congress shall assemble at least once in every year, and such meeting shall begin at noon on the 3d day of January, unless they shall by law appoint a different day.

SECTION 3. If, at the time fixed for the beginning of the term of the President, the President elect shall have died, the Vice President elect shall become President. If a President shall not have been chosen before the time fixed for the beginning of his term, or if the President elect shall have failed to qualify, then the Vice President elect shall act as President until a President shall have qualified; and the Congress may by law provide for the case wherein neither a President elect nor a Vice President elect shall have qualified, declaring who shall then act as President, or the manner in which one who is to act shall be selected, and such person shall act accordingly until a President or Vice President shall have qualified.

SECTION 4. The Congress may by law provide for the case of the death of any of the persons from whom the House of Representatives may choose a President whenever the right of choice shall have devolved upon them, and for the case of the death of any of the persons from whom the Senate may choose a Vice President whenever the right of choice shall have devolved upon them.

SECTION 5. Sections 1 and 2 shall take effect on the 15th day of October following the ratification of this article.

SECTION 6. This article shall be inoperative unless it shall have been ratified as an amendment to the Constitution by the legislatures of three-fourths of the several States within seven years from the date of its submission.

AMENDMENT XXI.

SECTION 1. The eighteenth article of amendment to the Constitution of the United States is hereby repealed.

SECTION 2. The transportation or importation into any State, Territory, or possession of the United States for delivery or use therein of intoxicating liquors, in violation of the laws thereof, is hereby prohibited.

SECTION 3. This article shall be inoperative unless it shall have been ratified as an amendment to the Constitution by conventions in the several States, as provided in the Constitution, within seven years from the date of the submission hereof to the States by the Congress.

AMENDMENT XXII.

SECTION 1. No person shall be elected to the office of the President more than twice, and no person who has held the office of President, or acted as President, for more than two years of a term to which some other person was elected President shall be elected to the office of the President more than once. But this Article shall not apply to any person holding the office of President when this Article was proposed by the Congress, and shall not prevent any person who may be holding the office of President, or acting as President, during the term within which this Article becomes operative from holding the office of President or acting as President during the remainder of such term.

SECTION 2. This Article shall be inoperative unless it shall have been ratified as an amendment to the Constitution by the legislatures of three-fourths of the several States within seven years from the date of its submission to the States by the Congress.

AMENDMENT XXIII.

SECTION 1. The District constituting the seat of Government of the United States shall appoint in such manner as the Congress may direct:

A number of electors of President and Vice President equal to the whole number of Senators and Representatives in Congress to which the District would be entitled if it were a State, but in no event more than the least populous State; they shall be in addition to those appointed by the States, but they shall be considered, for the purposes of the election of President and Vice President, to be electors appointed by a State; and they shall meet in the District and perform such duties as provided by the twelfth article of amendment.

SECTION 2. The Congress shall have power to enforce this article by appropriate legislation.

AMENDMENT XXIV.

SECTION 1. The right of citizens of the United States to vote in any primary or other election for President or Vice President, for electors for President or Vice President, or for Senator or Representative in Congress, shall not be denied or abridged by the United States or any State by reason of failure to pay any poll tax or other tax.

SECTION 2. The Congress shall have the power to enforce this article by appropriate legislation.

AMENDMENT XXV.

SECTION 1. In case of the removal of the President from office or of his death or resignation, the Vice President shall become President.

SECTION 2. Whenever there is a vacancy in the office of the Vice President, the President shall nominate a Vice President who shall take the office upon confirmation by a majority vote of both houses of Congress.

SECTION 3. Whenever the President transmits to the President pro tempore of the Senate and the Speaker of the House of Representatives his written declaration that he is unable to discharge the powers and duties of his office, and until he transmits to them a written declaration to the contrary, such powers and duties shall be discharged by the Vice President as Acting President.

SECTION 4. Whenever the Vice President and a majority of either the principal officers of the executive departments or of such other body as Congress may by law provide, transmit to the President pro tempore of the Senate and the Speaker of the House of Representatives their written declaration that the President is unable to discharge the powers and duties of his office, the Vice President shall immediately assume the powers and duties of the office as Acting President.

Thereafter when the President transmits to the President pro tempore of the Senate and the Speaker of the House of Representatives his written declaration that no inability exists, he shall resume the powers and duties of his office unless the Vice President and a majority of either the principal officers of the executive department or of such other body as Congress may by law provide, transmit within four days to the President pro tempore of the Senate and the Speaker of the House of Representatives their written declaration that the President is unable to discharge the powers and duties of his office. Thereupon Congress shall decide the issue, assembling within forty-eight hours for that purpose if not in session. If Congress within twenty-one days after receipt of the latter written declaration, or, if Congress is not in session, within twenty-one days after Congress is required to assemble, determines by two-thirds vote of both Houses that the President is unable to discharge the powers and duties of his office, the Vice President shall continue to discharge the same as Acting President; otherwise, the President shall resume the powers and duties of his office.

AMENDMENT XXVI.

SECTION 1. The right of citizens of the United States, who are 18 years of age or older, to vote shall not be denied or abridged by the United States or any state on account of age.

SECTION 2. The Congress shall have the power to enforce this article by appropriate legislation.

INDEX